Habitats in the United States, Grade K

What if you could challenge your kindergarten students to compare their local habitats with other habitats in the United States? With this volume in the *STEM Road Map Curriculum Series,* you can! *Habitats in the United States* outlines a journey that will steer your students toward authentic problem solving while grounding them in integrated STEM disciplines. Like the other volumes in the series, this book is designed to meet the growing need to infuse real-world learning into K–12 classrooms.

This interdisciplinary, three-lesson module uses project- and problem-based learning to help students look at their own neighborhood, city, state, and beyond to learn about the geography and habitats of various regions of the United States. Students will gather information on habitats and their similarities and differences based on weather, climate, and the animals, plants, and people residing there, to develop a reference manual for local zoo officials reorganizing their animal displays.

To support this goal, students will do the following:

- Explain that there are different types of habitats in different parts of the U.S.
- Explain how various habitats sustain animals and plants
- Identify climatic characteristics of several habitats
- Apply their knowledge of habitats to develop a reference guide about habitats in the U.S.
- Utilize technology to gather research information and communicate
- Identify technological advances and tools that scientists use to learn about sustainable systems
- Design and construct models of habitats
- Understand local weather patterns and make connections among weather patterns and plant and animal life where they live

The *STEM Road Map Curriculum Series* is anchored in the Next Generation Science Standards, the Common Core State Standards, and the Framework for 21st Century Learning. In-depth and flexible, *Habitats in the United States* can be used as a whole unit or in part to meet the needs of districts, schools, and teachers who are charting a course toward an integrated STEM approach.

Carla C. Johnson is a Professor of Science Education and Office of Research and Innovation Faculty Research Fellow at North Carolina State University, North Carolina, USA.

Janet B. Walton is a Senior Research Scholar at North Carolina State University's College of Education in Raleigh, North Carolina, USA.

Erin E. Peters-Burton is the Donna R. and David E. Sterling Endowed Professor in Science Education at George Mason University in Fairfax, Virginia, USA.

THE STEM ROAD MAP CURRICULUM SERIES

Series editors: Carla C. Johnson, Janet B. Walton, and Erin E. Peters-Burton

Map out a journey that will steer your students toward authentic problem solving as you ground them in integrated STEM disciplines.

Co-published by Routledge and NSTA Press, in partnership with the National Science Teaching Association, this K–12 curriculum series is anchored in the Next Generation Science Standards, the Common Core State Standards, and the Framework for 21st Century Learning. It was developed to meet the growing need to infuse real-world STEM learning into classrooms.

Each book is an in-depth module that uses project- and problem-based learning. First, your students are presented with a challenge. Then, they apply what they learn using science, social studies, English language arts, and mathematics. Engaging and flexible, each volume can be used as a whole unit or in part to meet the needs of districts, schools, and teachers who are charting a course toward an integrated STEM approach.

Modules are available from NSTA Press and Routledge, and organized under the following themes. For an update listing of the volumes in the series, please visit https://www.routledge.com/STEM-Road-Map-Curriculum-Series/book-series/SRM (for titles co-published by Routledge and NSTA Press), or www.nsta.org/book-series/stem-road-map-curriculum (for titles published by NSTA Press).

Co-published by Routledge and NSTA Press:

Optimizing the Human Experience:

- *Our Changing Environment, Grade K: STEM Road Map for Elementary School*
- *Genetically Modified Organisms, Grade 7: STEM Road Map for Middle School*
- *Rebuilding the Natural Environment, Grade 10: STEM Road Map for High School*
- *Mineral Resources, Grade 11: STEM Road Map for High School*

Cause and Effect:

- *Formation of the Earth, Grade 9: STEM Road Map for High School*

Sustainable Systems:

- *Habitats in the United States, Grade K: STEM Road Map for Elementary School*
- *Habitats Local and Far Away, Grade 1: STEM Road Map for Elementary School*
- *Hydropower Efficiency, Grade 4: STEM Road Map for Elementary School*
- *Composting, Grade 5: STEM Road Map for Elementary School*
- *Global Population Issues, Grade 7: STEM Road Map for Middle School*
- *The Speed of Green, Grade 8: STEM Road Map for Middle School*
- *Creating Global Bonds, Grade 12: STEM Road Map for High School*

Published by NSTA Press:

Innovation and Progress:

- *Amusement Park of the Future, Grade 6: STEM Road Map for Middle School*
- *Transportation in the Future, Grade 3: STEM Road Map for Elementary School*
- *Harnessing Solar Energy, Grade 4: STEM Road Map for Elementary School*
- *Wind Energy, Grade 5: STEM Road Map for Elementary School*
- *Construction Materials, Grade 11: STEM Road Map for High School*

The Represented World:

- *Patterns and the Plant World, Grade 1: STEM Road Map for Elementary School*
- *Investigating Environmental Changes, Grade 2: STEM Road Map for Elementary School*
- *Swing Set Makeover, Grade 3: STEM Road Map for Elementary School*
- *Rainwater Analysis, Grade 5: STEM Road Map for Elementary School*
- *Packaging Design, Grade 6: STEM Road Map for Middle School*
- *Improving Bridge Design, Grade 8: STEM Road Map for Middle School*
- *Radioactivity, Grade 11: STEM Road Map for High School*
- *Car Crashes, Grade 12: STEM Road Map for High School*

Cause and Effect:

- *Physics in Motion, Grade K: STEM Road Map for Elementary School*
- *Influence of Waves, Grade 1: STEM Road Map for Elementary School*
- *Natural Hazards, Grade 2: STEM Road Map for Elementary School*
- *Human Impacts on Our Climate, Grade 6: STEM Road Map for Middle School*
- *The Changing Earth, Grade 8: STEM Road Map for Middle School*
- *Healthy Living, Grade 10: STEM Road Map for High School*

Habitats in the United States, Grade K

STEM Road Map for Elementary School

Edited by Carla C. Johnson, Janet B. Walton, and Erin E. Peters-Burton

Designed cover image: © Shutterstock

First published 2024
by Routledge
605 Third Avenue, New York, NY 10158

and by Routledge
4 Park Square, Milton Park, Abingdon, Oxon OX14 4RN

Routledge is an imprint of the Taylor & Francis Group, an informa business

A co-publication with NSTA Press

© 2024 selection and editorial matter, National Science Teaching Association; individual chapters, the contributors

The right of Carla C. Johnson, Janet B. Walton, and Erin E. Peters-Burton to be identified as the authors of the editorial material, and of the authors for their individual chapters, has been asserted in accordance with sections 77 and 78 of the Copyright, Designs and Patents Act 1988.

All rights reserved. The purchase of this copyright material confers the right on the purchasing institution to photocopy pages which bear the copyright line at the bottom of the page. No other parts of this book may be reprinted or reproduced or utilised in any form or by any electronic, mechanical, or other means, now known or hereafter invented, including photocopying and recording, or in any information storage or retrieval system, without permission in writing from the publishers.

Routledge is committed to publishing material that promotes the best in inquiry-based science education. However, conditions of actual use may vary, and the safety procedures and practices described in this book are intended to serve only as a guide. Additional precautionary measures may be required. Routledge and the authors do not warrant or represent that the procedures and practices in this book meet any safety code or standard of federal, state, or local regulations. Routledge and the authors disclaim any liability for personal injury or damage to property arising out of or relating to the use of this book, including any of the recommendations, instructions, or materials contained therein.

Trademark notice: Product or corporate names may be trademarks or registered trademarks, and are used only for identification and explanation without intent to infringe.

Library of Congress Cataloging-in-Publication Data
Names: Johnson, Carla C., 1969– editor. | Walton, Janet B., 1968– editor. | Peters-Burton, Erin E., editor.
Title: Habitats in the United States, grade K : STEM road map for elementary school / edited by Carla C. Johnson, Janet B. Walton, and Erin E. Peters-Burton.
Description: New York, NY : Routledge, 2024. | Series: STEM road map curriculum | Includes bibliographical references and index.
Identifiers: LCCN 2023042207 (print) | LCCN 2023042208 (ebook) | ISBN 9781032579245 (hardback) | ISBN 9781032579252 (paperback) | ISBN 9781003441632 (ebook)
Subjects: LCSH: Habitat (Ecology)—Study and teaching (Elementary)—United States. | Kindergarten—Activity programs—United States. | Habitat (Ecology)—Study and teaching (Elementary)—Activity programs—United States. | Habitat (Ecology)—Study and teaching (Primary)—United States. | Ecology—Study and teaching (Elementary)—Activity programs.
Classification: LCC QH541.2 .H335 2024 (print) | LCC QH541.2 (ebook) | DDC 577.071—dc23/eng/20231222
LC record available at https://lccn.loc.gov/2023042207
LC ebook record available at https://lccn.loc.gov/2023042208

ISBN: 978-1-032-57924-5 (hbk)
ISBN: 978-1-032-57925-2 (pbk)
ISBN: 978-1-003-44163-2 (ebk)

DOI: 10.4324/9781003441632

Typeset in Palatino LT Std
by Apex CoVantage, LLC

CONTENTS

About the Editors and Authors ix

Acknowledgments xi

Part 1: The STEM Road Map: Background, Theory, and Practice

1. Overview of the *STEM Road Map Curriculum Series* 1
Carla C. Johnson, Erin E. Peters-Burton, and Tamara J. Moore

Standards-Based Approach 2

Themes in the *STEM Road Map Curriculum Series* 2

The Need for an Integrated STEM Approach 5

Framework for STEM Integration in the Classroom 6

The Need for the *STEM Road Map Curriculum Series* 7

References 7

2. Strategies Used in the *STEM Road Map Curriculum Series* 9
Erin E. Peters-Burton, Carla C. Johnson, Toni A. May, and Tamara J. Moore

Project- and Problem-Based Learning 9

Engineering Design Process 9

Learning Cycle 11

STEM Research Notebook 12

The Role of Assessment in the *STEM Road Map Curriculum Series* 13

Self-Regulated Learning Theory in the STEM Road Map Modules 16

Safety in STEM 18

References 19

Part 2: Habitats in the United States: STEM Road Map Module

3. Habitats in the U.S. Module Overview 23
Vanessa B. Morrison, Andrea R. Milner, Janet B. Walton, Carla C. Johnson, and Erin E. Peters-Burton

Module Summary 23

CONTENTS

Established Goals and Objectives 23

Challenge or Problem for Students to Solve:
  The Zoo Habitat Challenge 24

Content Standards Addressed in This STEM Road Map Module 24

STEM Research Notebook 24

Module Launch 25

Prerequisite Skills for the Module 25

Potential STEM Misconceptions 27

Self-Regulated Learning (SRL) Process Components 27

Strategies for Differentiating Instruction Within This Module 29

Strategies for English Language Learners (ELLS) 30

Safety Considerations for the Activities in This Module 31

Desired Outcomes and Monitoring Success 31

Assessment Plan Overview and Map 31

Module Timeline 34

Resources 37

References 37

4 Habitats in the U.S. Lesson Plans 39
Vanessa B. Morrison, Andrea R. Milner, Janet B. Walton, Carla C. Johnson, and Erin E. Peters-Burton

Lesson Plan 1: Amazing Habitats! 39

Lesson Plan 2: Let's Explore Our Local Habitat! 61

Lesson Plan 3: Let's Explore Habitats Throughout
  the United States! 80

Lesson Plan 4: The Zoo Habitat Challenge 91

CONTENTS

5 **Transforming Learning with Habitats in the U.S. and the *STEM Road Map Curriculum Series*** 113
Carla C. Johnson

Appendix A: STEM Research Notebook Templates 115

Appendix B: Observation, STEM Research Notebook, and Participation Rubric 143

Appendix C: Content Standards Addressed in this Module 145

Index 151

ABOUT THE EDITORS AND AUTHORS

Dr. Carla C. Johnson is a Professor of Science Education and Office of Research and Innovation Faculty Research Fellow at NC State University. Dr. Johnson has served (2015–2021) as the director of research and evaluation for the Department of Defense–funded Army Educational Outreach Program (AEOP), a global portfolio of STEM education programs, competitions, and apprenticeships. She has been a leader in STEM education for the past decade, serving as the director of STEM centers, editor of the School Science and Mathematics journal, and lead researcher for the evaluation of Tennessee's Race to the Top–funded STEM portfolio. Dr. Johnson has published over 200 articles, books, book chapters, and curriculum books focused on STEM education. She is a former science and social studies teacher and was the recipient of the 2013 Outstanding Science Teacher Educator of the Year award from the Association for Science Teacher Education (ASTE), the 2012 Award for Excellence in Integrating Science and Mathematics from the School Science and Mathematics Association (SSMA), the 2014 award for best paper on Implications of Research for Educational Practice from ASTE, and the 2006 Outstanding Early Career Scholar Award from SSMA. Her research focuses on STEM education policy implementation, effective science teaching, and integrated STEM approaches.

Dr. Janet B. Walton is a senior research scholar at NC State University's College of Education in Raleigh, North Carolina. Her research focuses includes collaboration between schools and community stakeholders for STEM education, problem- and project- based learning pedagogies, online learning, and mixed methods research methodologies. She leverages a background in workforce development along with her experience in curriculum development to bring contextual STEM experiences into the classroom and provide students and educators with innovative resources and curricular materials. She has served as the director of evaluation of research and evaluation for the Department of Defense–funded Army Educational Outreach Program (AEOP), a global portfolio of STEM education programs, competitions, and apprenticeships, and specializes in evaluation of STEM programs.

Dr. Erin E. Peters-Burton is the Donna R. and David E. Sterling endowed professor in science education at George Mason University in Fairfax, Virginia. She uses her experiences from 15 years as an engineer and secondary science, engineering,

ABOUT THE EDITORS AND AUTHORS

and mathematics teacher to develop research projects that directly inform classroom practice in science and engineering. Her research agenda is based on the idea that all students should build self-awareness of how they learn science and engineering. She works to help students see themselves as "science- minded" and help teachers create classrooms that support student skills to develop scientific knowledge. To accomplish this, she pursues research projects that investigate ways that students and teachers can use self-regulated learning theory in science and engineering, as well as how inclusive STEM schools can help students succeed. She received the Outstanding Science Teacher Educator of the Year award from ASTE in 2016 and a Teacher of Distinction Award and a Scholarly Achievement Award from George Mason University in 2012, and in 2010 she was named University Science Educator of the Year by the Virginia Association of Science Teachers.

Dr. Toni A. May is an associate professor of assessment, research, and statistics in the School of Education at Drexel University in Philadelphia. Dr. May's research concentrates on assessment and evaluation in education, with a focus on K–12 STEM.

Dr. Andrea R. Milner is the vice president and dean of academic affairs and an associate professor in the Teacher Education Department at Adrian College in Adrian, Michigan. A former early childhood and elementary teacher, Dr. Milner researches the effects constructivist classroom contextual factors have on student motivation and learning strategy use.

Dr. Tamara J. Moore is an associate professor of engineering education in the College of Engineering at Purdue University. Dr. Moore's research focuses on defining STEM integration through the use of engineering as the connection and investigating its power for student learning.

Dr. Vanessa B. Morrison is an associate professor in the Teacher Education Department at Adrian College. She is a former early childhood teacher and reading and language arts specialist whose research is focused on learning and teaching within a transdisciplinary framework.

ACKNOWLEDGMENTS

This module was developed as a part of the STEM Road Map project (Carla C. Johnson, principal investigator). The Purdue University College of Education, General Motors, and other sources provided funding for this project.

Copyright © 2015 from *STEM Road Map: A Framework for Integrated STEM Education*, edited by C. C. Johnson, E. E. Peters-Burton, and T. J. Moore. Reproduced by permission of Taylor and Francis Group, LLC, a division of Informa plc.

See www.routledge.com/9780367467524 for more information about *STEM Road Map: A Framework for Integrated STEM Education*.

PART 1

THE STEM ROAD MAP

BACKGROUND, THEORY, AND PRACTICE

OVERVIEW OF THE *STEM ROAD MAP CURRICULUM SERIES*

Carla C. Johnson, Erin E. Peters-Burton, and Tamara J. Moore

The *STEM Road Map Curriculum Series* was conceptualized and developed by a team of STEM educators from across the United States in response to a growing need to infuse real-world learning contexts, delivered through authentic problem-solving pedagogy, into K–12 classrooms. The curriculum series is grounded in integrated STEM, which focuses on the integration of the STEM disciplines—science, technology, engineering, and mathematics—delivered across content areas, incorporating the Framework for 21st Century Learning along with grade-level-appropriate academic standards. The curriculum series begins in kindergarten, with a five-week instructional sequence that introduces students to the STEM themes and gives them grade-level-appropriate topics and real-world challenges or problems to solve. The series uses project-based and problem-based learning, presenting students with the problem or challenge during the first lesson, and then teaching them science, social studies, English language arts, mathematics, and other content, as they apply what they learn to the challenge or problem at hand.

Authentic assessment and differentiation are embedded throughout the modules. Each *STEM Road Map Curriculum Series* module has a lead discipline, which may be science, social studies, English language arts, or mathematics. All disciplines are integrated into each module, along with ties to engineering. Another key component is the use of STEM Research Notebooks to allow students to track their own learning progress. The modules are designed with a scaffolded approach, with increasingly complex concepts and skills introduced as students progress through grade levels.

The developers of this work view the curriculum as a resource that is intended to be used either as a whole or in part to meet the needs of districts, schools, and teachers who are implementing an integrated STEM approach. A variety of implementation formats are possible, from using one stand-alone module at a given grade level to using all five modules to provide 25 weeks of instruction. Also, within each grade band (K–2, 3–5, 6–8, 9–12), the modules can be sequenced in various ways to suit specific needs.

Overview of the *STEM Road Map Curriculum Series*

STANDARDS-BASED APPROACH

The *STEM Road Map Curriculum Series* is anchored in the *Next Generation Science Standards* (*NGSS*), the *Common Core State Standards for Mathematics* (*CCSS Mathematics*), the *Common Core State Standards for English Language Arts* (*CCSS ELA*), and the Framework for 21st Century Learning. Each module includes a detailed curriculum map that incorporates the associated standards from the particular area correlated to lesson plans. The STEM Road Map has very clear and strong connections to these academic standards, and each of the grade-level topics was derived from the mapping of the standards to ensure alignment among topics, challenges or problems, and the required academic standards for students. Therefore, the curriculum series takes a standards-based approach and is designed to provide authentic contexts for application of required knowledge and skills.

THEMES IN THE *STEM ROAD MAP CURRICULUM SERIES*

The K–12 STEM Road Map is organized around five real-world STEM themes that were generated through an examination of the big ideas and challenges for society included in STEM standards and those that are persistent dilemmas for current and future generations:

- Cause and Effect
- Innovation and Progress
- The Represented World
- Sustainable Systems
- Optimizing the Human Experience

These themes are designed as springboards for launching students into an exploration of real-world learning situated within big ideas. Most important, the five STEM Road Map themes serve as a framework for scaffolding STEM learning across the K–12 continuum.

The themes are distributed across the STEM disciplines so that they represent the big ideas in science (Cause and Effect; Sustainable Systems), technology (Innovation and Progress; Optimizing the Human Experience), engineering (Innovation and Progress; Sustainable Systems; Optimizing the Human Experience), and mathematics (The Represented World), as well as concepts and challenges in social studies and 21st century skills that are also excellent contexts for learning in English language arts. The process of developing themes began with the clustering of the *NGSS* performance expectations and the National Academy of Engineering's grand challenges for engineering, which led to the development of the challenge in each module and connections of the module activities to the *CCSS Mathematics* and *CCSS ELA* standards. We

Overview of the STEM Road Map Curriculum Series

performed these mapping processes with large teams of experts and found that these five themes provided breadth, depth, and coherence to frame a high-quality STEM learning experience from kindergarten through 12th grade.

Cause and Effect

The concept of cause and effect is a powerful and pervasive notion in the STEM fields. It is the foundation of understanding how and why things happen as they do. Humans spend considerable effort and resources trying to understand the causes and effects of natural and designed phenomena to gain better control over events and the environment and to be prepared to react appropriately. Equipped with the knowledge of a specific cause-and-effect relationship, we can lead better lives or contribute to the community by altering the cause, leading to a different effect. For example, if a person recognizes that irresponsible energy consumption leads to global climate change, that person can act to remedy his or her contribution to the situation. Although cause and effect is a core idea in the STEM fields, it can actually be difficult to determine. Students should be capable of understanding not only when evidence points to cause and effect but also when evidence points to relationships but not direct causality. The major goal of education is to foster students to be empowered, analytic thinkers, capable of thinking through complex processes to make important decisions. Understanding causality, as well as when it cannot be determined, will help students become better consumers, global citizens, and community members.

Innovation and Progress

One of the most important factors in determining whether humans will have a positive future is innovation. Innovation is the driving force behind progress, which helps create possibilities that did not exist before. Innovation and progress are creative entities, but in the STEM fields, they are anchored by evidence and logic, and they use established concepts to move the STEM fields forward. In creating something new, students must consider what is already known in the STEM fields and apply this knowledge appropriately. When we innovate, we create value that was not there previously and create new conditions and possibilities for even more innovations. Students should consider how their innovations might affect progress and use their STEM thinking to change current human burdens to benefits. For example, if we develop more efficient cars that use byproducts from another manufacturing industry, such as food processing, then we have used waste productively and reduced the need for the waste to be hauled away, an indirect benefit of the innovation.

The Represented World

When we communicate about the world we live in, how the world works, and how we can meet the needs of humans, sometimes we can use the actual phenomena to

Overview of the *STEM Road Map Curriculum Series*

explain a concept. Sometimes, however, the concept is too big, too slow, too small, too fast, or too complex for us to explain using the actual phenomena, and we must use a representation or a model to help communicate the important features. We need representations and models such as graphs, tables, mathematical expressions, and diagrams because it makes our thinking visible. For example, when examining geologic time, we cannot actually observe the passage of such large chunks of time, so we create a timeline or a model that uses a proportional scale to visually illustrate how much time has passed for different eras. Another example may be something too complex for students at a particular grade level, such as explaining the p subshell orbitals of electrons to fifth graders. Instead, we use the Bohr model, which more closely represents the orbiting of planets and is accessible to fifth graders.

When we create models, they are helpful because they point out the most important features of a phenomenon. We also create representations of the world with mathematical functions, which help us change parameters to suit the situation. Creating representations of a phenomenon engages students because they are able to identify the important features of that phenomenon and communicate them directly. But because models are estimates of a phenomenon, they leave out some of the details, so it is important for students to evaluate their usefulness as well as their shortcomings.

Sustainable Systems

From an engineering perspective, the term *system* refers to the use of "concepts of component need, component interaction, systems interaction, and feedback. The interaction of subcomponents to produce a functional system is a common lens used by all engineering disciplines for understanding, analysis, and design" (Koehler, Bloom, and Binns 2013, p. 8). Systems can be either open (e.g., an ecosystem) or closed (e.g., a car battery). Ideally, a system should be sustainable, able to maintain equilibrium without much energy from outside the structure. Looking at a garden, we see flowers blooming, weeds sprouting, insects buzzing, and various forms of life living within its boundaries. This is an example of an ecosystem, a collection of living organisms that survive together, functioning as a system. The interaction of the organisms within the system and the influences of the environment (e.g., water, sunlight) can maintain the system for a period of time, thus demonstrating its ability to endure. Sustainability is a desirable feature of a system because it allows for existence of the entity in the long term.

In the STEM Road Map project, we identified different standards that we consider to be oriented toward systems that students should know and understand in the K–12 setting. These include ecosystems, the rock cycle, Earth processes (such as erosion, tectonics, ocean currents, weather phenomena), Earth-Sun-Moon cycles, heat transfer, and the interaction among the geosphere, biosphere, hydrosphere, and atmosphere. Students and teachers should understand that we live in a world of systems that are not independent of each other, but rather are intrinsically linked such that a disruption in one part of a system will have reverberating effects on other parts of the system.

Optimizing the Human Experience

Science, technology, engineering, and mathematics as disciplines have the capacity to continuously improve the ways humans live, interact, and find meaning in the world, thus working to optimize the human experience. This idea has two components: being more suited to our environment and being more fully human. For example, the progression of STEM ideas can help humans create solutions to complex problems, such as improving ways to access water sources, designing energy sources with minimal impact on our environment, developing new ways of communication and expression, and building efficient shelters. STEM ideas can also provide access to the secrets and wonders of nature. Learning in STEM requires students to think logically and systematically, which is a way of knowing the world that is markedly different from knowing the world as an artist. When students can employ various ways of knowing and understand when it is appropriate to use a different way of knowing or integrate ways of knowing, they are fully experiencing the best of what it is to be human. The problem based learning scenarios provided in the STEM Road Map help students develop ways of thinking like STEM professionals as they ask questions and design solutions. They learn to optimize the human experience by innovating improvements in the designed world in which they live.

THE NEED FOR AN INTEGRATED STEM APPROACH

At a basic level, STEM stands for science, technology, engineering, and mathematics. Over the past decade, however, STEM has evolved to have a much broader scope and implications. Now, educators and policy makers refer to STEM as not only a concentrated area for investing in the future of the United States and other nations but also as a domain and mechanism for educational reform.

The good intentions of the recent decade-plus of focus on accountability and increased testing has resulted in significant decreases not only in instructional time for teaching science and social studies but also in the flexibility of teachers to promote authentic, problem solving–focused classroom environments. The shift has had a detrimental impact on student acquisition of vitally important skills, which many refer to as 21st century skills, and often the ability of students to "think." Further, schooling has become increasingly siloed into compartments of mathematics, science, English language arts, and social studies, lacking any of the connections that are overwhelmingly present in the real world around children. Students have experienced school as content provided in boxes that must be memorized, devoid of any real-world context, and often have little understanding of why they are learning these things.

Overview of the *STEM Road Map Curriculum Series*

STEM-focused projects, curriculum, activities, and schools have emerged as a means to address these challenges. However, most of these efforts have continued to focus on the individual STEM disciplines (predominantly science and engineering) through more STEM classes and after-school programs in a "STEM enhanced" approach (Breiner et al. 2012). But in traditional and STEM enhanced approaches, there is little to no focus on other disciplines that are integral to the context of STEM in the real world. Integrated STEM education, on the other hand, infuses the learning of important STEM content and concepts with a much-needed emphasis on 21st century skills and a problem and project-based pedagogy that more closely mirrors the real-world setting for society's challenges. It incorporates social studies, English language arts, and the arts as pivotal and necessary (Johnson 2013; Rennie, Venville, and Wallace 2012; Roehrig et al. 2012).

FRAMEWORK FOR STEM INTEGRATION IN THE CLASSROOM

The *STEM Road Map Curriculum Series* is grounded in the Framework for STEM Integration in the Classroom as conceptualized by Moore, Guzey, and Brown (2014) and Moore et al. (2014). The framework has six elements, described in the context of how they are used in the *STEM Road Map Curriculum Series* as follows:

1. The STEM Road Map contexts are meaningful to students and provide motivation to engage with the content. Together, these allow students to have different ways to enter into the challenge.

2. The STEM Road Map modules include engineering design that allows students to design technologies (i.e., products that are part of the designed world) for a compelling purpose.

3. The STEM Road Map modules provide students with the opportunities to learn from failure and redesign based on the lessons learned.

4. The STEM Road Map modules include standards-based disciplinary content as the learning objectives.

5. The STEM Road Map modules include student-centered pedagogies that allow students to grapple with the content, tie their ideas to the context, and learn to think for themselves as they deepen their conceptual knowledge.

6. The STEM Road Map modules emphasize 21st century skills and, in particular, highlight communication and teamwork.

All of the STEM Road Map modules incorporate these six elements; however, the level of emphasis on each of these elements varies based on the challenge or problem in each module.

THE NEED FOR THE *STEM ROAD MAP CURRICULUM SERIES*

As focus is increasing on integrated STEM, and additional schools and programs decide to move their curriculum and instruction in this direction, there is a need for highquality, research-based curriculum designed with integrated STEM at the core. Several good resources are available to help teachers infuse engineering or more STEM enhanced approaches, but no curriculum exists that spans K–12 with an integrated STEM focus. The next chapter provides detailed information about the specific pedagogy, instructional strategies, and learning theory on which the *STEM Road Map Curriculum Series* is grounded.

REFERENCES

Breiner, J., M. Harkness, C. C. Johnson, and C. Koehler. 2012. What is STEM? A discussion about conceptions of STEM in education and partnerships. *School Science and Mathematics* 112 (1): 3–11.

Johnson, C. C. 2013. Conceptualizing integrated STEM education: Editorial. *School Science and Mathematics* 113 (8): 367–368.

Koehler, C. M., M. A. Bloom, and I. C. Binns. 2013. Lights, camera, action: Developing a methodology to document mainstream films' portrayal of nature of science and scientific inquiry. *Electronic Journal of Science Education* 17 (2).

Moore, T. J., S. S. Guzey, and A. Brown. 2014. Greenhouse design to increase habitable land: An engineering unit. *Science Scope* 51–57.

Moore, T. J., M. S. Stohlmann, H.-H. Wang, K. M. Tank, A. W. Glancy, and G. H. Roehrig. 2014. Implementation and integration of engineering in K–12 STEM education. In *Engineering in pre-college settings: Synthesizing research, policy, and practices*, eds. S. Purzer, J. Strobel, and M. Cardella, 35–60. West Lafayette, IN: Purdue Press.

Rennie, L., G. Venville, and J. Wallace. 2012. *Integrating science, technology, engineering, and mathematics: Issues, reflections, and ways forward*. New York: Routledge.

Roehrig, G. H., T. J. Moore, H. H. Wang, and M. S. Park. 2012. Is adding the *E* enough? Investigating the impact of K–12 engineering standards on the implementation of STEM integration. *School Science and Mathematics* 112 (1): 31–44.

STRATEGIES USED IN THE *STEM ROAD MAP CURRICULUM SERIES*

Erin E. Peters-Burton, Carla C. Johnson, Toni A. May, and Tamara J. Moore

The *STEM Road Map Curriculum Series* uses what has been identified through research as best-practice pedagogy, including embedded formative assessment strategies throughout each module. This chapter briefly describes the key strate-gies that are employed in the series.

PROJECT- AND PROBLEM-BASED LEARNING

Each module in the *STEM Road Map Curriculum Series* uses either project-based learning or problem-based learning to drive the instruction. Project-based learning begins with a driving question to guide student teams in addressing a contextualized local or community problem or issue. The outcome of project-based instruction is a product that is conceptualized, designed, and tested through a series of scaffolded learning experiences (Blumenfeld et al. 1991; Krajcik and Blumenfeld 2006). Problem-based learning is often grounded in a fictitious scenario, challenge, or problem (Barell 2006; Lambros 2004). On the first day of instruction within the unit, student teams are provided with the context of the problem. Teams work through a series of activities and use open-ended research to develop their potential solution to the problem or challenge, which need not be a tangible product (Johnson 2003).

ENGINEERING DESIGN PROCESS

The *STEM Road Map Curriculum Series* uses engineering design as a way to facilitate integrated STEM within the modules. The engineering design process (EDP) is depicted in Figure 2.1 (p. 10). It highlights two major aspects of engineering design—problem scoping and solution generation—and six specific components of working

Strategies Used in the *STEM Road Map Curriculum Series*

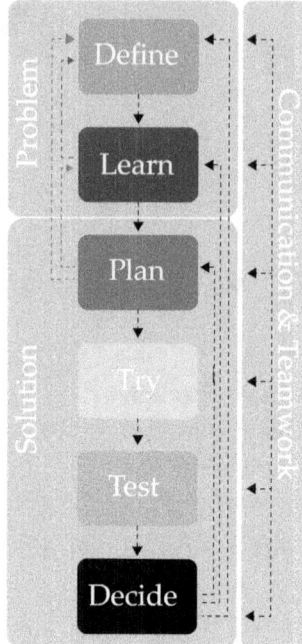

Figure 2.1. Engineering Design Process

Copyright © 2015 PictureSTEM-Purdue University Research Foundation

toward a design: define the problem, learn about the problem, plan a solution, try the solution, test the solution, decide whether the solution is good enough. It also shows that communication and teamwork are involved throughout the entire process. As the arrows in the figure indicate, the order in which the components of engineering design are addressed depends on what becomes needed as designers progress through the EDP. Designers must communicate and work in teams throughout the process. The EDP is iterative, meaning that components of the process can be repeated as needed until the design is good enough to present to the client as a potential solution to the problem.

Problem scoping is the process of gathering and analyzing information to deeply understand the engineering design problem. It includes defining the problem and learning about the problem. Defining the problem includes identifying the problem, the client, and the end user of the design. The client is the person (or people) who hired the designers to do the work, and the end user is the person (or people) who will use the final design. The designers must also identify the criteria and the constraints of the problem. The criteria are the things the client wants from the solution, and the constraints are the things that limit the possible solutions. The designers must spend significant time learning about the problem, which can include activities such as the following:

- Reading informational texts and researching about relevant concepts or contexts
- Identifying and learning about needed mathematical and scientific skills, knowledge, and tools
- Learning about things done previously to solve similar problems
- Experimenting with possible materials that could be used in the design

Problem scoping also allows designers to consider how to measure the success of the design in addressing specific criteria and staying within the constraints over multiple iterations of solution generation.

Solution generation includes planning a solution, trying the solution, testing the solution, and deciding whether the solution is good enough. Planning the solution includes generating many design ideas that both address the criteria and meet the constraints. Here the designers must consider what was learned about the problem during problem scoping. Design plans include clear communication of design ideas through media such as notebooks, blueprints, schematics, or storyboards. They also include details about the design, such as measurements, materials, colors, costs of materials, instructions for how things fit together, and sets of directions. Making the decision about which design idea to move forward involves considering the trade-offs of each design idea.

Once a clear design plan is in place, the designers must try the solution. Trying the solution includes developing a prototype (a testable model) based on the plan generated. The prototype might be something physical or a process to accomplish a goal. This component of design requires that the designers consider the risk involved in implementing the design. The prototype developed must be tested. Testing the solution includes conducting fair tests that verify whether the plan is a solution that is good enough to meet the client and end user needs and wants. Data need to be collected about the results of the tests of the prototype, and these data should be used to make evidence-based decisions regarding the design choices made in the plan. Here, the designers must again consider the criteria and constraints for the problem.

Using the data gathered from the testing, the designers must decide whether the solution is good enough to meet the client and end user needs and wants by assessment based on the criteria and constraints. Here, the designers must justify or reject design decisions based on the background research gathered while learning about the problem and on the evidence gathered during the testing of the solution. The designers must now decide whether to present the current solution to the client as a possibility or to do more iterations of design on the solution. If they decide that improvements need to be made to the solution, the designers must decide if there is more that needs to be understood about the problem, client, or end user; if another design idea should be tried; or if more planning needs to be conducted on the same design. One way or another, more work needs to be done.

Throughout the process of designing a solution to meet a client's needs and wants, designers work in teams and must communicate to each other, the client, and likely the end user. Teamwork is important in engineering design because multiple perspectives and differing skills and knowledge are valuable when working to solve problems. Communication is key to the success of the designed solution. Designers must communicate their ideas clearly using many different representations, such as text in an engineering notebook, diagrams, flowcharts, technical briefs, or memos to the client.

LEARNING CYCLE

The same format for the learning cycle is used in all grade levels throughout the STEM Road Map, so that students engage in a variety of activities to learn about phenomena in the modules thoroughly and have consistent experiences in the problem-and project-based learning modules. Expectations for learning by younger students are

Strategies Used in the *STEM Road Map Curriculum Series*

not as high as for older students, but the format of the progression of learning is the same. Students who have learned with curriculum from the STEM Road Map in early grades know what to expect in later grades. The learning cycle consists of five parts—Introductory Activity/Engagement, Activity/Exploration, Explanation, Elaboration/Application of Knowledge, and Evaluation/Assessment—and is based on the empirically tested 5E model from BSCS (Bybee et al. 2006).

In the Introductory Activity/Engagement phase, teachers introduce the module challenge and use a unique approach designed to pique students' curiosity. This phase gets students to start thinking about what they already know about the topic and begin wondering about key ideas. The Introductory Activity/Engagement phase positions students to be confident about what they are about to learn, because they have prior knowledge, and clues them into what they don't yet know.

In the Activity/Exploration phase, the teacher sets up activities in which students experience a deeper look at the topics that were introduced earlier. Students engage in the activities and generate new questions or consider possibilities using preliminary investigations. Students work independently, in small groups, and in whole-group settings to conduct investigations, resulting in common experiences about the topic and skills involved in the real-world activities. Teachers can assess students' development of concepts and skills based on the common experiences during this phase.

During the Explanation phase, teachers direct students' attention to concepts they need to understand and skills they need to possess to accomplish the challenge. Students participate in activities to demonstrate their knowledge and skills to this point, and teachers can pinpoint gaps in student knowledge during this phase.

In the Elaboration/Application of Knowledge phase, teachers present students with activities that engage in higher-order thinking to create depth and breadth of student knowledge, while connecting ideas across topics within and across STEM. Students apply what they have learned thus far in the module to a new context or elaborate on what they have learned about the topic to a deeper level of detail.

In the last phase, Evaluation/Assessment, teachers give students summative feedback on their knowledge and skills as demonstrated through the challenge. This is not the only point of assessment (as discussed in the section on Embedded Formative Assessments), but it is an assessment of the culmination of the knowledge and skills for the module. Students demonstrate their cognitive growth at this point and reflect on how far they have come since the beginning of the module. The challenges are designed to be multidimensional in the ways students must collaborate and communicate their new knowledge.

STEM RESEARCH NOTEBOOK

One of the main components of the *STEM Road Map Curriculum Series* is the STEM Research Notebook, a place for students to capture their ideas, questions, observations,

Strategies Used in the *STEM Road Map Curriculum Series* 2

reflections, evidence of progress, and other items associated with their daily work. At the beginning of each module, the teacher walks students through the setup of the STEM Research Notebook, which could be a three-ring binder, composition book, or spiral notebook. You may wish to have students create divided sections so that they can easily access work from various disciplines during the module. Electronic notebooks kept on student devices are also acceptable and encouraged. Students will develop their own table of contents and create chapters in the notebook for each module.

Each lesson in the *STEM Road Map Curriculum Series* includes one or more prompts that are designed for inclusion in the STEM Research Notebook and appear as questions or statements that the teacher assigns to students. These prompts require students to apply what they have learned across the lesson to solve the big problem or challenge for that module. Each lesson is designed to meaningfully refer students to the larger problem or challenge they have been assigned to solve with their teams. The STEM Research Notebook is designed to be a key formative assessment tool, as students' daily entries provide evidence of what they are learning. The notebook can be used as a mechanism for dialogue between the teacher and students, as well as for peer and self-evaluation.

The use of the STEM Research Notebook is designed to scaffold student notebooking skills across the grade bands in the *STEM Road Map Curriculum Series*. In the early grades, children learn how to organize their daily work in the notebook as a way to collect their products for future reference. In elementary school, students structure their notebooks to integrate background research along with their daily work and lesson prompts. In the upper grades (middle and high school), students expand their use of research and data gathering through team discussions to more closely mirror the work of STEM experts in the real world.

THE ROLE OF ASSESSMENT IN THE *STEM ROAD MAP CURRICULUM SERIES*

Starting in the middle years and continuing into secondary education, the word *assessment* typically brings grades to mind. These grades may take the form of a letter or a percentage, but they typically are used as a representation of a student's content mastery. If well thought out and implemented, however, classroom assessment can offer teachers, parents, and students valuable information about student learning and misconceptions that does not necessarily come in the form of a grade (Popham 2013).

The *STEM Road Map Curriculum Series* provides a set of assessments for each module. Teachers are encouraged to use assessment information for more than just assigning grades to students. Instead, assessments of activities requiring students to actively engage in their learning, such as student journaling in STEM Research Notebooks, collaborative presentations, and constructing graphic organizers, should be used to move student learning forward. Whereas other curriculum with assessments may include

Strategies Used in the *STEM Road Map Curriculum Series*

objective-type (multiple-choice or matching) tests, quizzes, or worksheets, we have intentionally avoided these forms of assessments to better align assessment strategies with teacher instruction and student learning techniques. Since the focus of this book is on project- or problem-based STEM curriculum and instruction that focuses on higher-level thinking skills, appropriate and authentic performance assessments were developed to elicit the most reliable and valid indication of growth in student abilities (Brookhart and Nitko 2008).

Comprehensive Assessment System

Assessment throughout all STEM Road Map curriculum modules acts as a comprehensive system in which formative and summative assessments work together to provide teachers with high-quality information on student learning. Formative assessment occurs when the teacher finds out formally or informally what a student knows about a smaller, defined concept or skill and provides timely feedback to the student about his or her level of proficiency. Summative assessments occur when students have performed all activities in the module and are given a cumulative performance evaluation in which they demonstrate their growth in learning.

A comprehensive assessment system can be thought of as akin to a sporting event. Formative assessments are the practices: It is important to accomplish them consistently, they provide feedback to help students improve their learning, and making mistakes can be worthwhile if students are given an opportunity to learn from them. Summative assessments are the competitions: Students need to be prepared to perform at the best of their ability. Without multiple opportunities to practice skills along the way through formative assessments, students will not have the best chance of demonstrating growth in abilities through summative assessments (Black and Wiliam 1998).

Embedded Formative Assessments

Formative assessments in this module serve two main purposes: to provide feedback to students about their learning and to provide important information for the teacher to inform immediate instructional needs. Providing feedback to students is particularly important when conducting problem- or project-based learning because students take on much of the responsibility for learning, and teachers must facilitate student learning in an informed way. For example, if students are required to conduct research for the Activity/Exploration phase but are not familiar with what constitutes a reliable resource, they may develop misconceptions based on poor information. When a teacher monitors this learning through formative assessments and provides specific feedback related to the instructional goals, students are less likely to develop incomplete or incorrect conceptions in their independent investigations. By using formative assessment to detect problems in student learning and then acting on this information, teachers help move student learning forward through these teachable moments.

Strategies Used in the *STEM Road Map Curriculum Series*

Formative assessments come in a variety of formats. They can be informal, such as asking students probing questions related to student knowledge or tasks or simply observing students engaged in an activity to gather information about student skills. Formative assessments can also be formal, such as a written quiz or a laboratory practical. Regardless of the type, three key steps must be completed when using formative assessments (Sondergeld, Bell, and Leusner 2010). First, the assessment is delivered to students so that teachers can collect data. Next, teachers analyze the data (student responses) to determine student strengths and areas that need additional support. Finally, teachers use the results from information collected to modify lessons and create learning environments that reinforce weak points in student learning. If student learning information is not used to modify instruction, the assessment cannot be considered formative in nature. Formative assessments can be about content, science process skills, or even learning skills. When a formative assessment focuses on content, it assesses student knowledge about the disciplinary core ideas from the *Next Generation Science Standards* (*NGSS*) or content objectives from *Common Core State Standards for Mathematics* (*CCSS Mathematics*) or *Common Core State Standards for English Language Arts* (*CCSS ELA*). Content-focused formative assessments ask students questions about declarative knowledge regarding the concepts they have been learning. Process skills formative assessments examine the extent to which a student can perform science and engineering practices from the *NGSS* or process objectives from *CCSS Mathematics* or *CCSS ELA*, such as constructing an argument. Learning skills can also be assessed formatively by asking students to reflect on the ways they learn best during a module and identify ways they could have learned more.

Assessment Maps

Assessment maps or blueprints can be used to ensure alignment between classroom instruction and assessment. If what students are learning in the classroom is not the same as the content on which they are assessed, the resultant judgment made on student learning will be invalid (Brookhart and Nitko 2008). Therefore, the issue of instruction and assessment alignment is critical. The assessment map for this book (found in Chapter 3) indicates by lesson whether the assessment should be completed as a group or on an individual basis, identifies the assessment as formative or summative in nature, and aligns the assessment with its corresponding learning objectives.

Note that the module includes far more formative assessments than summative assessments. This is done intentionally to provide students with multiple opportunities to practice their learning of new skills before completing a summative assessment. Note also that formative assessments are used to collect information on only one or two learning objectives at a time so that potential relearning or instructional modifications can focus on smaller and more manageable chunks of information. Conversely, summative assessments in the module cover many more learning objectives,

2 Strategies Used in the *STEM Road Map Curriculum Series*

as they are traditionally used as final markers of student learning. This is not to say that information collected from summative assessments cannot or should not be used formatively. If teachers find that gaps in student learning persist after a summative assessment is completed, it is important to revisit these existing misconceptions or areas of weakness before moving on (Black et al. 2003).

SELF-REGULATED LEARNING THEORY IN THE STEM ROAD MAP MODULES

Many learning theories are compatible with the STEM Road Map modules, such as constructivism, situated cognition, and meaningful learning. However, we feel that the self-regulated learning theory (SRL) aligns most appropriately (Zimmerman 2000). SRL requires students to understand that thinking needs to be motivated and managed (Ritchhart, Church, and Morrison 2011). The STEM Road Map modules are student centered and are designed to provide students with choices, concrete hands-on experiences, and opportunities to see and make connections, especially across subjects (Eliason and Jenkins 2012; NAEYC 2016). Additionally, SRL is compatible with the modules because it fosters a learning environment that supports students' motivation, enables students to become aware of their own learning strategies, and requires reflection on learning while experiencing the module (Peters and Kitsantas 2010).

The theory behind SRL (see Figure 2.2) explains the different processes that students engage in before, during, and after a learning task. Because SRL is a cyclical learning process, the accomplishment of one cycle develops strategies for the next learning cycle. This cyclic way of learning aligns with the various sections in the STEM Road Map lesson plans on Introductory Activity/Engagement, Activity/Exploration, Explanation, Elaboration/Application of Knowledge, and Evaluation/Assessment. Since the students engaged in a module take on much of the responsibility for learning, this theory also provides guidance for teachers to keep students on the right track.

Figure 2.2. SRL Theory

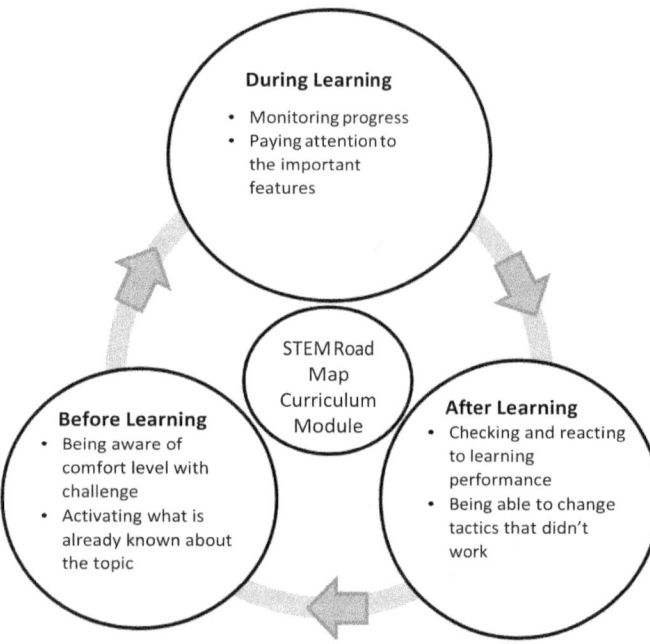

Source: Adapted from Zimmerman 2000.

NATIONAL SCIENCE TEACHING ASSOCIATION

Strategies Used in the *STEM Road Map Curriculum Series*

The remainder of this section explains how SRL theory is embedded within the five sections of each module and points out ways to support students in becoming independent learners of STEM while productively functioning in collaborative teams.

Before Learning: Setting the Stage

Before attempting a learning task such as the STEM Road Map modules, teachers should develop an understanding of their students' level of comfort with the process of accomplishing the learning and determine what they already know about the topic. When students are comfortable with attempting a learning task, they tend to take more risks in learning and as a result achieve deeper learning (Bandura 1986).

The STEM Road Map curriculum modules are designed to foster excitement from the very beginning. Each module has an Introductory Activity/Engagement section that introduces the overall topic from a unique and exciting perspective, engaging the students to learn more so that they can accomplish the challenge. The Introductory Activity also has a design component that helps teachers assess what students already know about the topic of the module. In addition to the deliberate designs in the lesson plans to support SRL, teachers can support a high level of student comfort with the learning challenge by finding out if students have ever accomplished the same kind of task and, if so, asking them to share what worked well for them.

During Learning: Staying the Course

Some students fear inquiry learning because they aren't sure what to do to be successful (Peters 2010). However, the STEM Road Map curriculum modules are embedded with tools to help students pay attention to knowledge and skills that are important for the learning task and to check student understanding along the way. One of the most important processes for learning is the ability for learners to monitor their own progress while performing a learning task (Peters 2012). The modules allow students to monitor their progress with tools such as the STEM Research Notebooks, in which they record what they know and can check whether they have acquired a complete set of knowledge and skills. The STEM Road Map modules support inquiry strategies that include previewing, questioning, predicting, clarifying, observing, discussing, and journaling (Morrison and Milner 2014). Through the use of technology throughout the modules, inquiry is supported by providing students access to resources and data while enabling them to process information, report the findings, collaborate, and develop 21st century skills.

It is important for teachers to encourage students to have an open mind about alternative solutions and procedures (Milner and Sondergeld 2015) when working through the STEM Road Map curriculum modules. Novice learners can have difficulty knowing what to pay attention to and tend to treat each possible avenue for information as equal (Benner 1984). Teachers are the mentors in a classroom and can point out ways

Strategies Used in the *STEM Road Map Curriculum Series*

for students to approach learning during the Activity/Exploration, Explanation, and Elaboration/Application of Knowledge portions of the lesson plans to ensure that students pay attention to the important concepts and skills throughout the module. For example, if a student is to demonstrate conceptual awareness of motion when working on roller coaster research, but the student has misconceptions about motion, the teacher can step in and redirect student learning.

After Learning: Knowing What Works

The classroom is a busy place, and it may often seem that there is no time for self-reflection on learning. Although skipping this reflective process may save time in the short term, it reduces the ability to take into account things that worked well and things that didn't so that teaching the module may be improved next time. In the long run, SRL skills are critical for students to become independent learners who can adapt to new situations. By investing the time it takes to teach students SRL skills, teachers can save time later, because students will be able to apply methods and approaches for learning that they have found effective to new situations. In the Evaluation/Assessment portion of the STEM Road Map curriculum modules, as well as in the formative assessments throughout the modules, two processes in the after-learning phase are supported: evaluating one's own performance and accounting for ways to adapt tactics that didn't work well. Students have many opportunities to self-assess in formative assessments, both in groups and individually, using the rubrics provided in the modules.

The designs of the *NGSS* and *CCSS* allow for students to learn in diverse ways, and the STEM Road Map curriculum modules emphasize that students can use a variety of tactics to complete the learning process. For example, students can use STEM Research Notebooks to record what they have learned during the various research activities. Notebook entries might include putting objectives in students' own words, compiling their prior learning on the topic, documenting new learning, providing proof of what they learned, and reflecting on what they felt successful doing and what they felt they still needed to work on. Perhaps students didn't realize that they were supposed to connect what they already knew with what they learned. They could record this and would be prepared in the next learning task to begin connecting prior learning with new learning.

SAFETY IN STEM

Student safety is a primary consideration in all subjects but is an area of particular concern in science, where students may interact with unfamiliar tools and materials that may pose additional safety risks. It is important to implement safety practices within the context of STEM investigations, whether in a classroom laboratory or in the field. When you keep safety in mind as a teacher, you avoid many potential issues with the lesson while also protecting your students.

Strategies Used in the *STEM Road Map Curriculum Series*

STEM safety practices encompass things considered in the typical science classroom. Ensure that students are familiar with basic safety considerations, such as wearing protective equipment (e.g., safety glasses or goggles and latex-free gloves) and taking care with sharp objects, and know emergency exit procedures. Teachers should learn beforehand the locations of the safety eyewash, fume hood, fire extinguishers, and emergency shut-off switch in the classroom and how to use them. Also be aware of any school or district safety policies that are in place and apply those that align with the work being conducted in the lesson. It is important to review all safety procedures annually.

STEM investigations should always be supervised. Each lesson in the modules includes teacher guidelines for applicable safety procedures that should be followed. Before each investigation, teachers should go over these safety procedures with the student teams. Some STEM focus areas such as engineering require that students can demonstrate how to properly use equipment in the maker space before the teacher allows them to proceed with the lesson.

Information about classroom science safety, including a safety checklist for science classrooms, general lab safety recommendations, and links to other science safety resources, is available at the Council of State Science Supervisors (CSSS) website at *www.csss-science. org/safety.shtml*. The National Science Teachers Association (NSTA) provides a list of science rules and regulations, including standard operating procedures for lab safety, and a safety acknowledgement form for students and parents or guardians to sign. You can access these resources at *http://static.nsta.org/pdfs/Safety InTheScienceClassroom.pdf*. In addition, NSTA's Safety in the Science Classroom web page (www.nsta.org/safety) has numerous links to safety resources, including papers written by the NSTA Safety Advisory Board.

Disclaimer: The safety precautions for each activity are based on use of the recommended materials and instructions, legal safety standards, and better professional practices. Using alternative materials or procedures for these activities may jeopardize the level of safety and therefore is at the user's own risk.

REFERENCES

Bandura, A. 1986. *Social foundations of thought and action: A social cognitive theory*. Englewood Cliffs, NJ: Prentice-Hall.

Barell, J. 2006. *Problem-based learning: An inquiry approach*. Thousand Oaks, CA: Corwin Press.

Benner, P. 1984. *From novice to expert: Excellence and power in clinical nursing practice*. Menlo Park, CA: Addison-Wesley Publishing Company.

Black, P., C. Harrison, C. Lee, B. Marshall, and D. Wiliam. 2003. *Assessment for learning: Putting it into practice*. Berkshire, UK: Open University Press.

Black, P., and D. Wiliam. 1998. Inside the black box: Raising standards through classroom assessment. *Phi Delta Kappan* 80 (2): 139–148.

Strategies Used in the *STEM Road Map Curriculum Series*

Blumenfeld, P., E. Soloway, R. Marx, J. Krajcik, M. Guzdial, and A. Palincsar. 1991. Motivating project-based learning: Sustaining the doing, supporting learning. *Educational Psychologist* 26 (3): 369–398.

Brookhart, S. M., and A. J. Nitko. 2008. *Assessment and grading in classrooms.* Upper Saddle River, NJ: Pearson.

Bybee, R., J. Taylor, A. Gardner, P. Van Scotter, J. Carlson, A. Westbrook, and N. Landes. 2006. *The BSCS 5E instructional model: Origins and effectiveness. http://science.education.nih.gov/houseofreps. nsf/b82d55fa138783c2852572c9004f5566/$FILE/Appendix?D.pdf.*

Eliason, C. F., and L. T. Jenkins. 2012. *A practical guide to early childhood curriculum.* 9th ed. New York: Merrill.

Johnson, C. 2003. Bioterrorism is real-world science: Inquiry-based simulation mirrors real life. *Science Scope* 27 (3): 19–23.

Krajcik, J., and P. Blumenfeld. 2006. Project-based learning. In *The Cambridge handbook of the learning sciences,* ed. R. Keith Sawyer, 317–334. New York: Cambridge University Press.

Lambros, A. 2004. *Problem-based learning in middle and high school classrooms: A teacher's guide to implementation.* Thousand Oaks, CA: Corwin Press.

Milner, A. R., and T. Sondergeld. 2015. Gifted urban middle school students: The inquiry continuum and the nature of science. *National Journal of Urban Education and Practice* 8 (3): 442–461.

Morrison, V., and A. R. Milner. 2014. Literacy in support of science: A closer look at cross-curricular instructional practice. *Michigan Reading Journal* 46 (2): 42–56.

National Association for the Education of Young Children (NAEYC). 2016. Developmentally appropriate practice position statements. *www.naeyc.org/positionstatements/dap.*

Peters, E. E. 2010. Shifting to a student-centered science classroom: An exploration of teacher and student changes in perceptions and practices. *Journal of Science Teacher Education* 21 (3): 329–349.

Peters, E. E. 2012. Developing content knowledge in students through explicit teaching of the nature of science: Influences of goal setting and self-monitoring. *Science and Education* 21 (6): 881–898.

Peters, E. E., and A. Kitsantas. 2010. The effect of nature of science metacognitive prompts on science students' content and nature of science knowledge, metacognition, and self-regulatory efficacy. *School Science and Mathematics* 110: 382–396.

Popham, W. J. 2013. *Classroom assessment: What teachers need to know.* 7th ed. Upper Saddle River, NJ: Pearson.

Ritchhart, R., M. Church, and K. Morrison. 2011. *Making thinking visible: How to promote engagement, understanding, and independence for all learners.* San Francisco, CA: Jossey-Bass.

Sondergeld, T. A., C. A. Bell, and D. M. Leusner. 2010. Understanding how teachers engage in formative assessment. *Teaching and Learning* 24 (2): 72–86.

Zimmerman, B. J. 2000. Attaining self-regulation: A social-cognitive perspective. In *Handbook of self-regulation,* ed. M. Boekaerts, P. Pintrich, and M. Zeidner, 13–39. San Diego: Academic Press.

PART 2

HABITATS IN THE UNITED STATES

STEM ROAD MAP MODULE

HABITATS IN THE U.S. MODULE OVERVIEW

Vanessa B. Morrison, Andrea R. Milner, Janet B. Walton, Carla C. Johnson, and Erin E. Peters-Burton

THEME: Sustainable Systems

LEAD DISCIPLINES: Science and Social Studies

MODULE SUMMARY

This module introduces students to the concept of habitats and challenges students to compare their local habitats with other habitats in the United States. Students will look at their own neighborhood, city, and state and beyond to learn about the geography and habitats of various regions of the United States (adapted from Koehler, Bloom, and Milner, 2015).

ESTABLISHED GOALS AND OBJECTIVES

At the conclusion of this module, students will be able to do the following:

- Explain that there are different types of habitats in different parts of the U.S.
- Identify several habitats in the U.S.
- Explain how various habitats sustain animals and plants
- Identify climatic characteristics of several habitats
- Compare and contrast features of different habitats
- Apply their knowledge of habitats to develop a reference guide about habitats in the U.S.
- Utilize technology to gather research information and communicate
- Identify technological advances and tools that scientists use to learn about sustainable systems

3

Habitats in the U.S. Module Overview

- Design and construct models of habitats
- Understand local weather patterns and make connections among weather patterns and plant and animal life where they live

CHALLENGE OR PROBLEM FOR STUDENTS TO SOLVE: THE ZOO HABITAT CHALLENGE

In this module, student teams are challenged to help zoo officials convert their zoo displays so that displays are grouped by habitats. Students will be presented with a scenario for a zoo in which different types of animals are currently grouped together (for example, all big cats are grouped in one area); however, the zoo wishes to create a new layout in which animals are grouped together by habitat and needs information to help them do this. Students will develop a reference manual to be used by the zoo that describes various U.S. habitats and their similarities and differences in terms of weather, climate, and the animals, and plants that live in those habitats.

CONTENT STANDARDS ADDRESSED IN THIS STEM ROAD MAP MODULE

A full listing with descriptions of the standards this module addresses can be found in Appendix C. Listings of the particular standards addressed within lessons are provided in a table for each lesson in Chapter 4.

STEM RESEARCH NOTEBOOK

Each student should maintain a STEM Research Notebook, which will serve as a place for students to organize their work throughout this module (see pp. 12–13 for more general discussion on setup and use of this notebook). All written work in the module should be included in the notebook, including records of students' thoughts and ideas, fictional accounts based on the concepts in the module, and records of student progress through the EDP. The notebooks may be maintained across subject areas, giving students the opportunity to see that although their classes may be separated during the school day, the knowledge they gain is connected. Templates for the STEM Research Notebook pages for this module are included in Appendix A.

Emphasize to students the importance of organizing all information in a Research Notebook. Explain to them that scientists and other researchers maintain detailed Research Notebooks in their work. These notebooks, which are crucial to researchers' work because they contain critical information and track the researchers' progress, are often considered legal documents for scientists who are pursuing patents or wish to provide proof of their discovery process.

Habitats in the U.S. Module Overview

MODULE LAUNCH

Following agreed-on rules for discussions, launch the module by holding a class discussion about habitats, asking students these questions:

- What are habitats?
- Are there different types of habitats?
- What kinds of habitats are there?
- Are habitats the same everywhere?
- Where and when have you seen various habitats?

Then, have students explore habitats by watching a video about animal habitats such as "What is a Habitat?" at *www.youtube.com/watch?v=ZrSWYE37MJs*.

PREREQUISITE SKILLS FOR THE MODULE

Students enter this module with a wide range of preexisting skills, information, and knowledge. Table 3.1 provides an overview of prerequisite skills and knowledge that students are expected to apply in this module, along with examples of how they apply this knowledge throughout the module. Differentiation strategies are also provided for students who may need additional support in acquiring or applying this knowledge.

Table 3.1. Prerequisite Key Knowledge and Examples of Applications and Differentiation

Prerequisite Key Knowledge	Application of Knowledge	Differentiation for Students Needing Knowledge
Science		
• A basic understanding of cause-and-effect relationships	• Students will determine how components of habitats such as climate and animal and plant life are interdependent	Science: • Provide demonstrations of cause and effect (for example, dropping egg [cause] and observing breakage [effect], emphasizing that cause is why something happens, effect is what happens) • Read-aloud picture books to class and have students identify cause-and-effect sequences • Create a class T-chart to record causes and related effects students observe in the classroom and in literature

continued

Habitats in the U.S. Module Overview

Table 3.1. (*continued*)

Prerequisite Key Knowledge	Application of Knowledge	Differentiation for Students Needing Knowledge
Mathematics		
• Basic numeracy skills • An understanding that measurements are ways to describe objects and phenomena	• Students will read temperatures with assistance and record temperatures • Students will describe components of habitats numerically	• Model measurement techniques using standard and nonstandard units of measurement • Read-aloud nonfiction texts about temperature and measurement to class • Provide opportunities for students to practice measurement and counting in a variety of settings (for example, in the classroom and outdoors)
English Language Arts		
• Make predictions and express those predictions orally and in writing or drawings • Ask and respond to questions	• Students will make and confirm or reject predictions • Students will share their thought processes through notebooking and asking and responding to questions	• Practice making predictions as a class when reading fictional texts • Model the process of using information and prior knowledge to make predictions • Read out instructions on STEM Research Notebook pages • Where students are asked to write words, write the word on the board for students to copy or provide an outline of the word that students can trace and have them glue it into the appropriate place in their notebooks • Provide samples of notebook entries
• Basic speaking and listening skills	• Students will participate in whole-class discussions • Students will engage in collaborative group discussions in the development of their reference guide and in completing group tasks throughout the module	• Model speaking and listening skills • Create a class list of good listening and good speaking practices • Read picture books that feature collaboration and teamwork

POTENTIAL STEM MISCONCEPTIONS

Students enter the classroom with a wide variety of prior knowledge and ideas, so it is important to be alert to misconceptions, or inappropriate understandings of foundational knowledge. These misconceptions can be classified as one of several types: "preconceived notions," opinions based on popular beliefs or understandings; "nonscientific beliefs," knowledge students have gained about science from sources outside the scientific community; "conceptual misunderstandings," incorrect conceptual models based on incomplete understanding of concepts; "vernacular misconceptions," misunderstandings of words based on their common use versus their scientific use; and "factual misconceptions," incorrect or imprecise knowledge learned in early life that remains unchallenged (NRC 1997, p. 28). Misconceptions must be addressed and dismantled in order for students to reconstruct their knowledge, and therefore teachers should be prepared to take the following steps:

- *Identify students' misconceptions.*
- *Provide a forum for students to confront their misconceptions.*
- *Help students reconstruct and internalize their knowledge, based on scientific models.* (NRC 1997, p. 29)

Keeley and Harrington (2010) recommend using diagnostic tools such as probes and formative assessment to identify and confront student misconceptions and begin the process of reconstructing student knowledge. Keeley and Harrington's *Uncovering Student Ideas in Science* series contains probes targeted toward uncovering student misconceptions in a variety of areas and may be a useful resource for addressing student misconceptions in this module. In addition, Know, Want to Know, Learned (KWL) charts are used throughout this module. These charts are completed as a class, and will provide useful information about students' existing knowledge and misconceptions regarding lesson concepts.

Some commonly held misconceptions specific to lesson content are provided with each lesson so that you can be alert for student misunderstanding of the science concepts presented and used during this module.

SELF-REGULATED LEARNING (SRL) PROCESS COMPONENTS

Table 3.2 illustrates some of the activities in the Habitats in the U.S. module and how they align to the SRL processes before, during, and after learning. See chapter 2 (pp. 16–18) for an overview of SRL theory.

3 Habitats in the U.S. Module Overview

Table 3.2. SRL Learning Components

Learning Process Components	Example from Habitats in the U.S. Module	Lesson Number and Learning Component
Before Learning		
Motivates students	Students watch a video to help them access and organize their prior knowledge about habitats	Lesson 1 Introductory Activity/ Engagement
Evokes prior learning	Students brainstorm and record their ideas as a class about what they know about the needs of living things; guiding questions are presented to evoke prior knowledge	Lesson 1 Activity/Investigation
During Learning		
Focuses on important features	Students will investigate habitats through two activities: the Our Neighborhood Habitat investigation (walking tour of the school neighborhood) and the Shelter Me activity (designing a human shelter); throughout the activities, students record their findings and ideas	Lesson 2 Activity/Investigation
Helps students monitor their progress	Teachers use guiding questions and the STEM Research Notebook as a formative assessment of student knowledge	Lesson 2 Activity/Investigation
After Learning		
Evaluates learning	Students create and present a Habitat Reference Guide. Teachers can use this manual as a summative assessment of students' understanding of habitats in the U.S.	Lesson 4 Activity/Investigation
Takes account of what worked and what did not work	Students can reflect on their performance from the teacher's feedback and/or students can fill out the rubric with the help of the teacher to self-assess their performance	Lesson 4 Evaluation/Assessment

Habitats in the U.S. Module Overview

STRATEGIES FOR DIFFERENTIATING INSTRUCTION WITHIN THIS MODULE

For the purposes of this curriculum module, differentiated instruction is conceptualized as a way to tailor instruction—including process, content, and product—to various student needs in your class. A number of differentiation strategies are integrated into lessons across the module. The problem- and project-based learning approach used in the lessons is designed to address students' multiple intelligences by providing a variety of entry points and methods to investigate the key concepts in the module (for example, investigating habitats via scientific inquiry, literature, journaling, and collaborative design). Differentiation strategies for students needing support in prerequisite knowledge can be found in Table 3.1 (p. 25). You are encouraged to use information gained about student prior knowledge during introductory activities and discussions to inform your instructional differentiation. Strategies incorporated into this lesson include flexible grouping, varied environmental learning contexts, assessments, compacting, tiered assignments and scaffolding, and mentoring.

Flexible Grouping: Students work collaboratively in a variety of activities throughout this module. Grouping strategies: you might employ include student-led grouping, grouping students according to ability level or common interests, grouping students randomly, or grouping them so that students in each group have complementary strengths (for instance, one student might be strong in mathematics, another in art, and another in writing).

Varied Environmental Learning Contexts: Students have the opportunity to learn in various contexts throughout the module, including alone, in groups, in quiet reading and research-oriented activities, and in active learning through inquiry and design activities. In addition, students learn in a variety of ways, including through doing inquiry activities, journaling, reading a variety of texts, watching videos, participating in class discussion, and conducting web-based research.

Assessments: Students are assessed in a variety of ways throughout the module, including individual and collaborative formative and summative assessments. Students have the opportunity to produce work via written text, oral presentations, and modeling.

Compacting: Based on student prior knowledge, you may wish to adjust instructional activities for students who exhibit prior mastery of a learning objective. Since student work in science is largely collaborative throughout the module, this strategy may be most appropriate for mathematics, social studies, or ELA activities.

Tiered Assignments and Scaffolding: Based on your awareness of student ability, understanding of concepts, and mastery of skills, you may wish to provide students with variations on activities by adding complexity to assignments or providing more or fewer learning supports for activities throughout the module. For instance, some

Habitats in the U.S. Module Overview

students may need additional support in identifying key search words and phrases for web-based research or may benefit from cloze sentence handouts to enhance vocabulary understanding. Other students may benefit from expanded reading selections and additional reflective writing or from working with manipulatives and other visual representations of mathematical concepts. You may also work with your school librarian to compile a classroom database of research resources and supplementary readings for different reading levels and on a variety of topics related to the module challenge to provide opportunities for students to undertake independent reading.

Mentoring: As group design teamwork becomes increasingly complex throughout the module, you may wish to have a resource teacher, older student, or volunteer work with groups that struggle to stay on task and collaborate effectively.

STRATEGIES FOR ENGLISH LANGUAGE LEARNERS (ELLS)

Students who are developing proficiency in English language skills require additional supports to simultaneously learn academic content and the specialized language associated with specific content areas. WIDA has created a framework for providing support to these students and makes available rubrics and guidance on differentiating instructional materials for multilingual learners (see *www.wida.us*). In particular, multilingual learners may benefit from additional sensory supports such as images, physical modeling, and graphic representations of module content, as well as interactive support through collaborative work. This module incorporates a variety of sensory supports and offers ongoing opportunities for ELL students to work with collaboratively.

Teachers differentiating instruction for multilingual learners should carefully consider the needs of these students as they introduce and use academic language in various language domains (listening, speaking, reading, and writing) throughout this module. To adequately differentiate instruction for ELL students, teachers should have an understanding of the proficiency level of each student. The following five overarching preK–5 WIDA learning standards are relevant to this module:

> Standard 1: Social and Instructional Language. Focus on following directions, personal information, collaboration with peers.
>
> Standard 2: The language of Language Arts. Focus on non-fiction, fiction, sequence of story, elements of story.
>
> Standard 3: The language of Mathematics. Focus on basic operations, number sense, interpretation of data, patterns.
>
> Standard 4: The language of Science. Focus on forces in nature, scientific process, living and nonliving things, organisms and environment.

Habitats in the U.S. Module Overview

Standard 5: The language of Social Studies. Focus on homes and habitats, jobs and careers, geography, representations of Earth (maps and globes).

SAFETY CONSIDERATIONS FOR THE ACTIVITIES IN THIS MODULE

Science activities in this module focus on exploring habitats and the living things found in habitats. Students will work with a variety of materials as they explore animals and habitats. You should discuss appropriate use of materials with students at the start of each activity. All laboratory occupants must wear safety glasses or goggles during all phases of inquiry activities (setup, hands-on investigation, and takedown) and laboratory floor surfaces must be kept dry to prevent slipping. For more general safety guidelines, see the Safety in STEM section in Chapter 2 (pp. 18–19) and for lesson-specific safety information, see the Safety Notes section of each lesson in Chapter 4.

DESIRED OUTCOMES AND MONITORING SUCCESS

The desired outcomes for this module are outlined in Table 3.3, along with suggested ways to gather evidence to monitor student success. For more specific details on desired outcomes, see the Established Goals and Objectives sections for the module and individual lessons.

Table 3.3. Desired Outcomes and Evidence of Success in Achieving Identified Outcomes

Desired Outcome	Evidence of Success	
	Performance Tasks	Other Measures
Students will understand and demonstrate their knowledge about animal homes and habitats by comparing and contrasting their local habitat with other habitats in various regions of the United States	• Student teams will develop dioramas of habitats • Students will develop reference manuals that describe various habitats and their similarities and differences.	Students are assessed using the Observation, STEM Research Notebook, and Participation Rubric

ASSESSMENT PLAN OVERVIEW AND MAP

Table 3.4 provides an overview of the major group and individual *products* and *deliverables*, or things that student teams will produce in this module, that constitute the assessment for this module. See Table 3.5 (p. 32) for a full assessment map of formative and summative assessments in this module.

Habitats in the United States, Grade K

Habitats in the U.S. Module Overview

Table 3.4. Major Products and Deliverables in Lead Disciplines for Groups and Individuals

Lesson	Major Group Products/Deliverables	Major Individual Products/Deliverables
1	• Wonder Worms Habitats	• STEM Research Notebook entries 1–6 • Lesson Assessment
2	• Our Neighborhood Habitats investigation • Shelter Me structures	• STEM Research Notebook entries 7–11 • Lesson Assessment
3	• My Dynamic Habitat Dioramas and presentations	• STEM Research Notebook entries 11–14 • Lesson Assessment
4	• My Habitat Reference Manual presentations	• My Habitat Reference Manual template

Table 3.5. Assessment Map for Habitats in the U.S. Module

Lesson	Assessment	Group/Individual	Formative/Summative	Lesson Objective Assessed
1	STEM Research Notebook *entries*	Individual	Formative	• Identify several habitats • Identify the basic needs of living things
1	Wonder Worms Worm Habitats *performance task*	Group	Formative	• Observe and describe animal behavior in various conditions
1	Lesson *assessment*	Individual	Summative	• Identify several habitats
2	STEM Research Notebook *entries*	Individual	Formative	• Identify the components of habitats as shelter, water, food, air, and space • Identify properties of their local habitat • Identify how the local habitat meets the needs of several types of animals and plants
2	Our Neighborhood Habitats Walk *performance task*	Group	Formative	• Identify properties of their local habitat • Identify how the local habitat meets the needs of several types of animals and plants • Use technology tools to gather data

Habitats in the U.S. Module Overview

Lesson	Assessment	Group/Individual	Formative/Summative	Lesson Objective Assessed
2	Shelter Me Structures *performance task*	Group	Formative	• Identify the steps of the EDP • Use the EDP to design and build a model of a shelter for human beings
2	Lesson *assessment*	Individual	Summative	• Identify the components of habitats as shelter, water, food, air, and space
3	My Dynamic Habitat Dioramas *performance task and presentations*	Group	Formative	• Use their understanding of characteristics of habitats to design and construct models of habitats
3	Lesson *assessment*	Individual	Summative	• Identify several habitats within the U.S. and describe characteristics of those habitats
4	Reference Guide for Habitats *template*	Individual	Summative	• Synthesize their learning about habitats to develop a reference guide about habitats in the U.S. • Compare and contrast various habitats in relation to climate, animals, and plants
4	Reference Guide for Habitats *presentation*	Group	Summative	• Synthesize their learning about habitats to develop a reference guide about habitats in the U.S. • Compare and contrast various habitats in relation to climate, animals, and plants • Present the information in their reference manuals to an audience

Habitats in the United States, Grade K

3 Habitats in the U.S. Module Overview

MODULE TIMELINE

Tables 3.6–3.10 provide lesson timelines for each week of the module. These timelines are provided for general guidance only and are based on class times of approximately 30 minutes.

Table 3.6. STEM Road Map Module Schedule Week One

Day 1 *Lesson 1* *Amazing Habitats!*	Day 2 *Lesson 1* *Amazing Habitats!*	Day 3 *Lesson 1* *Amazing Habitats!*	Day 4 *Lesson 1* *Amazing Habitats!*	Day 5 *Lesson 1* *Amazing Habitats!*
Launch the module Group discussion on habitats Show video about habitats	Introduce weather chart Begin class vocabulary chart	Introduce basic needs of living things with class discussion Show video about basic needs Conduct interactive read-aloud of *Animals at Home* by David Lock	Conduct interactive read aloud of *Wiggling Worms at Work* by Wendy Pfeffer Begin Wonder Worms activity (predict)	Continue Wonder Worms activity (observe and explain) Interactive read-aloud of *Guinea Pigs Add Up* by Margaret Cuyler

34   NATIONAL SCIENCE TEACHING ASSOCIATION

Habitats in the U.S. Module Overview

Table 3.7. STEM Road Map Module Schedule Week Two

Day 6	Day 7	Day 8	Day 9	Day 10
Lesson 1 Amazing Habitats!	*Lesson 2 Let's Explore Our Local Habitat!*	*Lesson 2 Let's Explore Our Local Habitat!*	*Lesson 2 Let's Explore Our Local Habitat!*	*Lesson 2 Let's Explore Our Local Habitat!*
Lesson assessment	Introduce students to the components of habitats	Conduct an interactive read-aloud related to local or regional habitats	Conduct Our Neighborhood Habitat investigation and discuss findings	Introduce Shelter Me activity and EDP
Students remove and count "worms" from boxes full of beans or beads	Students identify where they live on a U.S. map	Introduce Our Neighborhood Habitat investigation		Begin Shelter Me activity (define, learn)
	Show video highlighting habitats in the part of the U.S. where students live			Conduct interactive read-aloud of *The Great Graph Contest* by Loreen Leedy, graph findings from Our Neighborhood Habitat investigation

Table 3.8. STEM Road Map Module Schedule Week Three

Day 11	Day 12	Day 13	Day 14	Day 15
Lesson 2 Let's Explore Our Local Habitat!	*Lesson 2 Let's Explore Our Local Habitat!*	*Lesson 2 Let's Explore Our Local Habitat!*	*Lesson 2 Let's Explore Our Local Habitat!*	*Lesson 3 Let's Explore Habitats throughout the United States!*
Continue Shelter Me activity (plan, try, begin test)	Complete Shelter Me activity (finish test and present)	Conduct interactive read-aloud of *My Neighborhood: Places and Faces* by Lisa Bullard	Lesson assessment	Introduce and discuss two other habitats from different parts of the U.S.
	Conduct interactive read-aloud about a different habitat	Discuss how people's needs are met	Students practice comparing numbers	Show videos about the two habitats
	Compare and contrast habitats			

Habitats in the United States, Grade K

Habitats in the U.S. Module Overview

Table 3.9 STEM Road Map Module Schedule Week Four

Day 16	Day 17	Day 18	Day 19	Day 20
Lesson 3 Let's Explore Habitats throughout the United States!	*Lesson 3 Let's Explore Habitats throughout the United States!*	*Lesson 3 Let's Explore Habitats throughout the United States!*	*Lesson 3 Let's Explore Habitats throughout the United States!*	*Lesson 3 Let's Explore Habitats throughout the United States!*
Begin My Dynamic Habitat Diorama investigation – Diorama #1	Continue My Dynamic Habitat Diorama investigation – Diorama #1	Continue My Dynamic Habitat Diorama investigation – Diorama #2	Continue My Dynamic Habitat Diorama investigation – Diorama #2	Students share dioramas with the class Lesson assessment

Table 3.10. STEM Road Map Module Schedule Week Five

Day 21	Day 22	Day 23	Day 24	Day 25
The Zoo Habitat Challenge	*The Zoo Habitat Challenge*	*The Zoo Habitat Challenge*	*The Zoo Habitat Challenge*	*The Zoo Habitat Challenge*
Hold a class discussion about zoos and remind students of module challenge Conduct an interactive read-aloud of *My Visit to the Zoo* by Aliki	Students choose their habitats and begin work on Our Habitat Reference Guides	Students continue work on Our Habitat Reference Guides Discuss how people live differently in different habitats Conduct an interactive read-aloud of *The Berenstain Bears' Moving day* by Stan Berenstain	Students continue work on Our Habitat Reference Guides Discuss living things' impacts on the environment around them Conduct an interactive read-aloud of *On Our Nature Walk: Our First Talk About Our Impact on the Environment* by Jillian Roberts	Student teams present their Our Habitat Reference Guides to an audience of "zoo officials"

Habitats in the U.S. Module Overview

RESOURCES

The media specialist can help teachers locate resources for students to view and read about habitats, animals, plants, weather, and related content. Special educators and reading specialists can help find supplemental sources for students needing extra support in reading and writing. Additional resources may be found online. Community resources for this module may include biologists, botanists, and zoologists.

REFERENCES

Keeley, P., and R. Harrington. 2010. *Uncovering student ideas in physical science, volume 1: 45 new force and motion assessment probes.* Arlington, VA: NSTA Press.

Koehler, C., M. A. Bloom, and A. R. Milner. 2015. The STEM Road Map for grades K–2. In *STEM Road Map: A framework for integrated STEM education,* eds. C. C. Johnson, E. E. Peters-Burton, and T. J. Moore, 41–67. New York: Routledge. *www.routledge.com/products/9781138804234*

National Research Council (NRC). 1997. *Science teaching reconsidered: A handbook.* Washington, DC: National Academies Press.

WIDA. 2020. *WIDA English language development standards framework, 2020 edition: Kindergarten–grade 12.* Board of Regents of the University of Wisconsin System. *https://wida.wisc.edu/sites/default/files/resource/WIDA-ELD-Standards-Framework-2020.pdf*

HABITATS IN THE U.S. LESSON PLANS

Vanessa B. Morrison, Andrea R. Milner, Janet B. Walton, Carla C. Johnson, and Erin E. Peters-Burton

Lesson Plan 1: Amazing Habitats!

This lesson will introduce students to habitats as places where animals and plants live and will create and investigate worm habitats. Students will be introduced to the module challenge.

ESSENTIAL QUESTIONS

- What are habitats?
- Are there different types of habitats?
- What kinds of habitats are there?
- Are habitats the same everywhere?
- Where and when have you seen various habitats?

ESTABLISHED GOALS AND OBJECTIVES

At the conclusion of this lesson, students will be able to do the following:

- Identify several types of habitats
- Identify the basic needs of living things
- Observe and describe animal behavior in various conditions
- Describe and analyze patterns of local weather to make connections between weather and animal and plant life

4 Habitats in the U.S. Lesson Plans

TIME REQUIRED

Six days (approximately 30 minutes each; see Tables 3.6–3.7, pp. 34–35).

MATERIALS

Required Materials for Lesson 1

- STEM Research Notebooks (one per student, see pp. 12–13 for STEM Research Notebook information)
- Computer with internet access for viewing videos
- Books:
    o *Animals at Home* by David Lock
    o *Wiggling Worms at Work* by Wendy Pfeffer
    o *Guinea Pigs Add Up* by Margaret Cuyler
- Weather chart for the entire class (create or purchase) or handouts for each student (attached at the end of this lesson)
- Chart paper
- Markers
- U.S. map
- Pencils (one per student)
- Crayons for use in STEM Research Notebook entries (one set per student)

Additional Materials for Wonder Worms (per pair of students if students will work in pairs for this activity; see Preparation for Lesson 1, pp. 48–50, for more information):

- Two worms (red earthworms or night crawlers)
- Two clear two liter plastic bottles with the top three inches cut off
- Two opaque boxes or containers (with lids)
- Two clear plastic bottles with top three inches cut off
- Five paper towels
- Cup of water
- Soil (enough to cover the bottom of the bottle to a depth of about three–four inches)
- Sand (enough to cover the bottom of the bottle to a depth of about three–four inches)

Additional Materials for Mathematics Connection (per pair of students):

- plastic shoebox
- beans or plastic beads to fill box to within about one inch of the top
- Ten to 12 "worms" (plastic fishing worms or chenille stems)
- Pair of large plastic tweezers

SAFETY NOTES

1. Remind students that personal protective equipment (safety glasses or goggles, aprons, and gloves) must be worn during the setup, hands-on, and take-down segments of activities.

2. Caution students not to eat any materials used in activities.

3. Students should use caution when handling scissors, as the sharp points and blades can cut or puncture skin.

4. Tell students to be careful when handling containers. Cans and cut plastic may have sharp edges, which can cut or puncture skin. Glass or plastic bottles can break and cut skin.

5. Immediately wipe up any spilled water or soil on the floor to avoid a slip-and-fall hazard.

6. Have students wash hands with soap and water after activities are completed.

CONTENT STANDARDS AND KEY VOCABULARY

Table 4.1 lists the content standards from the *Next Generation Science Standards* (*NGSS*), *Common Core State Standards* (*CCSS*), and the Framework for 21st Century Learning that this lesson addresses, and Table 4.2 (pp. 44–45) presents the key vocabulary. Vocabulary terms are provided for both teacher and student use. Teachers may choose to introduce some or all of the terms to students.

Table 4.1. Standards Addressed in STEM Road Map Module Lesson 1

NEXT GENERATION SCIENCE STANDARDS
PERFORMANCE OBJECTIVES
• K-LS1–1. Use observations to describe patterns of what plants and animals (including humans) need to survive
• K-PS3–1. Make observations to determine the effect of sunlight on Earth's surface

Continued

Habitats in the U.S. Lesson Plans

Table 4.1. (*continued*)

DISCIPLINARY CORE IDEAS

LS1.C. *Organization for Matter and Energy Flow in Organisms*
- All animals need food in order to live and grow. They obtain their food from plants or from other animals. Plants need water and light to live and grow

ESS3.A. *Natural Resources*
- Living things need water, air, and resources from the land, and they live in places that have the things they need. Humans use natural resources for everything they do

PS3.B. *Conservation of Energy and Energy Transfer*
- Sunlight warms Earth's surface

CROSSCUTTING CONCEPTS

Patterns
- Patterns in the natural and human designed world can be observed and used as evidence

Systems and System Models
- Systems in the natural and designed world have parts that work together

Cause and Effect
- Events have causes that generate observable patterns

SCIENCE AND ENGINEERING PRACTICES

Analyzing and Interpreting Data
- Analyzing data in K-2 builds on prior experiences and progresses to collecting, recording, and sharing observations
- Use observations (firsthand or from media) to describe patterns in the natural world in order to answer scientific questions (K-LS1–1)

Developing and Using Models
- Modeling in K-2 builds on prior experiences and progresses to include using and developing models (i.e., diagram, drawing, physical replica, diorama, dramatization, storyboard) that represent concrete events or design solutions
- Use a model to represent relationships in the natural world

Planning and Carrying Out Investigations
- Planning and carrying out investigations to answer questions or test solutions to problems in K-2 builds on prior experiences and progresses to simple investigations, based on fair tests, which provide data to support explanations or design solutions
- Make observations (firsthand or from media) to collect data that can be used to make comparisons

COMMON CORE STATE STANDARDS FOR MATHEMATICS

MATHEMATICAL PRACTICES
- MP1. Make sense of problems and persevere in solving them
- MP2. Reason abstractly and quantitatively
- MP3. Construct viable arguments and critique the reasoning of others

Habitats in the U.S. Lesson Plans

- MP4. Model with mathematics
- MP5. Use appropriate tools strategically
- MP6. Attend to precision
- MP7. Look for and make use of structure
- MP8. Look for and express regularity in repeated reasoning

MATHEMATICAL CONTENT
- K.CC.B.4. Understand the relationship between numbers and quantities; connect counting to cardinality
- K.CC.B.4a. When counting objects, say the number names in the standard order, pairing each object with one and only one number name and each number name with one and only one object
- K.CC.B.4b. Understand that the last number name said tells the number of objects counted. The number of objects is the same regardless of their arrangement or the order in which they were counted
- K.CC.B.4c. Understand that each successive number name refers to a quantity that is one larger
- K.CC.C.6. Identify whether the number of objects in one group is greater than, less than, or equal to the number of objects in another group, for example, by using matching and counting strategies
- K.CC.C.7. Compare two numbers between 1 and 10 presented as written numerals
- K.MD.A.1. Describe measurable attributes of objects, such as length or weight. Describe several measurable attributes of a single object
- K.MD.A.2. Directly compare two objects with a measurable attribute in common, to see which object has "more of"/"less of" the attribute, and describe the difference. For example, directly compare the heights of two children and describe one child as taller/shorter
- K.MD.B.3. Classify objects into given categories; count the numbers of objects in each category and sort the categories by count

COMMON CORE STATE STANDARDS FOR ENGLISH LANGUAGE ARTS

READING STANDARDS
- RI.K.1. With prompting and support, ask and answer questions about key details in a text
- RI.K.3. With prompting and support, describe the connection between two individuals, events, ideas, or pieces of information in a text

WRITING STANDARDS
- W.K.2. Use a combination of drawing, dictating, and writing to compose informative/explanatory texts in which they name what they are writing about and supply some information about the topic
- W.K.5. With guidance and support from adults, respond to questions and suggestions from peers and add details to strengthen writing as needed
- W.K.7. Participate in shared research and writing projects (for example, explore a number of books by a favorite author and express opinions about them)

SPEAKING AND LISTENING STANDARDS
- SL.K.1. Participate in collaborative conversations with diverse partners about *kindergarten topics and texts* with peers and adults in small and larger groups

Continued

Habitats in the U.S. Lesson Plans

Table 4.1. (*continued*)

- SL.K.3. Ask and answer questions in order to seek help, get information, or clarify something that is not understood
- SL.K.5. Add drawings or other visual displays to descriptions as desired to provide additional detail

NATIONAL ASSOCIATION FOR THE EDUCATION OF YOUNG CHILDREN STANDARDS
- 2.G.02. Children are provided with varied opportunities and materials to learn key content and principles of science
- 2.G.03. Children are provided with varied opportunities and materials that encourage them to use the five senses to observe, explore, and experiment with scientific phenomena
- 2.G.04. Children are provided with varied opportunities to use simple tools to observe objects and scientific phenomena
- 2.G.05. Children are provided with varied opportunities and materials to collect data and to represent and document their findings (for example, through drawing or graphing)
- 2.G.06. Children are provided with varied opportunities and materials that encourage them to think, questions, and reason about observed and inferred phenomena
- 2.G.07. Children are provided with varied opportunities and materials that encourage them to discuss scientific concepts in everyday conversation
- 2.G.08. Children are provided with varied opportunities and materials that help them learn and use scientific terminology and vocabulary associated with the content areas
- 2.H.02. All children have opportunities to access technology that they can use
- 2.H.03. Technology is used to extend learning within the classroom and integrate and enrich the curriculum

FRAMEWORK FOR 21ST CENTURY LEARNING
- Interdisciplinary themes
- Learning and Innovation Skills
- Information, Media and Technology Skills
- Life and Career Skills

Table 4.2. Key Vocabulary in Lesson 1

Key Vocabulary	Definition
city	an area where many people live closely together and/or there are many businesses close together; there are many streets and roads and no farmland; a city is larger and busier than a town
climate	the weather conditions in an area over an extended period of time
coastal	describes an area at the edge of the ocean
desert	a hot, dry place that gets very little rain
earthworm	an animal that does not have a skeleton and that burrows in the soil
forest	a large area covered with trees where different plants grow and where animals live

Key Vocabulary	Definition
freshwater	a body of water that occurs naturally and is not salty like the ocean; lakes, streams, rivers, wetlands
grassland (or prairie)	a very large open place where most of the plants are grasses
habitat	a place in nature where plants and animals live and have their needs met
ocean	a very large body of salt water
town	an area where people live that is smaller than a city and less busy
urban	a word that describes a city
weather	the daily conditions in a particular area including temperature, precipitation, cloud cover, and air pressure
wetlands	an area of land that stays very wet for most of the year

TEACHER BACKGROUND INFORMATION

Kindergarteners are rapidly developing across all domains (physical, social and emotional, personality, cognitive, and language). They are beginning to develop logical thinking skills, the ability to reason out problems, autonomy, and growing independence. Throughout this module, you should support and facilitate the development of these domains within each student.

Giving students regular opportunities to share their ideas, discoveries, and questions, about scientific phenomena in a group setting can build kindergarteners' enthusiasm for topics, expand their perspectives, help them develop new ideas, and motivate them for scientific inquiry as well as helping them to build their language and communication skills. Asking open-ended questions about students' learning and ideas and encouraging them to make and share their observations are effective ways to engage kindergarteners in science talk, and allows opportunities for you to model using scientific language (terms associated with the concept being investigated) and practices (for example, observing, comparing, predicting, and measuring). In addition, this science talk can help you to identify misconceptions students may hold and provide opportunities for building new understanding. It may be helpful to work as a class to establish a set of guidelines or rules for this communication (for example, don't talk over another person who is speaking, be respectful of others' ideas even if we think they are wrong, look at the person talking, always ask questions when you have them).

Habitats

This module focuses on habitats in the United States. Habitats will be presented as communities in which plants and animals live and that provide the basic needs (water, food, shelter, air, and space) of the living things there. The focus of the module will be on habitats as encompassing animals' homes (for example, nests, houses) and the surrounding area and conditions. Students will learn that habitats in different parts of the

Habitats in the U.S. Lesson Plans

U.S. have different geographical and climate characteristics and that different types of plants and animals live in different habitats. The habitats presented in this module are grasslands or prairies, forests, deserts, oceans, freshwater bodies of water, coastal areas, and urban areas. The following websites provide additional information about habitats:

- *www.skyenimals.com/browse_habitat.cgi*
- *http://environment.nationalgeographic.com/environment/habitats/*

You will start each day of the module by redirecting students' attention to the module challenge (the Zoo Habitat Challenge). You may wish to incorporate interactive read-aloud about zoos (see Suggested Books section at the end of the chapter). In addition, a sample of a zoo map is included at the end of this lesson that you may wish to use to discuss with students how animals are grouped at zoos and how habitats are reproduced at zoos.

Earthworms

Students will explore earthworm habitats in this lesson. Earthworms are invertebrates with segmented bodies. They do not have skeletons, but have rings of muscles that allow them to move. The segments of earthworms' bodies are covered with tiny hairs that help them move through the soil in which they live. Earthworms do not have lungs; instead, they absorb oxygen through their skin. This explains why earthworms come to the surface of the ground during rainstorms, since, when the soil is saturated, earthworms are unable to absorb oxygen through their skin. They live in a variety of habitats in the U.S., although they do not live in deserts or in areas where the ground is frozen for much of the year. Earthworms are important for soil health since they tunnel through the soil, loosening it, and making it more suited for plant root growth and turning the soil, much as farmers do when they plow. In addition, earthworms' digestion systems excrete finely textured soil, and their excrement is nutrient rich. The two commonly encountered types of earthworms are red earthworms, typically found close to the surface of the soil, and night crawlers that usually live deeper in the soil. For more information about earthworms, see the following resources:

- *https://kids.nationalgeographic.com/animals/invertebrates/facts/earthworm*
- *www.sciencelearn.org.nz/resources/17-earthworm-adaptations*

Careers

In this module, students will be introduced to the idea that engineers and other STEM workers work together in teams to solve problems. Students will experience working in teams and in pairs as they progress through a simple scientific process including predicting, observing, and explaining phenomena related to forces in this lesson. This introduction to teamwork sets the stage for students' use of the engineering design process (EDP) later in the module.

Habitats in the U.S. Lesson Plans

You may also wish to connect students' work in this module with other careers such as the following (adapted from Koehler, Bloom, and Milner, 2015) suggest:

- ecologist
- geographer
- journalist
- mathematician
- meteorologist
- biologist
- botanist

For more information about these and other careers, see the Bureau of Labor Statistics' *Occupational Outlook Handbook* at *www.bls.gov/ooh/home.htm*.

Know, Want to Know, Learned (KWL) Charts

Throughout this module, you will track student knowledge on Know, Want to Know, Learned (KWL) charts. These charts will be used to access and assess student prior knowledge, encourage students to think critically about the topic under discussion, and track student learning throughout the module. Each chart should consist of three columns, labeled "What We Know," "What We Want to Know," and "What We Learned." Write the topic at the top of each chart. It may be helpful to post these charts in a prominent place in the classroom so that students can refer to them throughout the module. Students will include their personal know, want to know, and learned reflections in their STEM Research Notebooks entries.

Interactive Read-Alouds

This module also uses interactive read-alouds to engage students, access their prior knowledge, develop student background knowledge, and introduce topical vocabulary. These read-alouds expose children to teacher-read literature that may be beyond their independent reading levels but is consistent with their listening level. Interactive read-alouds may incorporate a variety of techniques, and you can find helpful information regarding these techniques at the following websites:

- *www.readingrockets.org/article/repeated-interactive-read-alouds-preschool-and-kindergarten*
- *www.readwritethink.org/professional-development/strategy-guides/teacher-read-aloud-that-30799.html*

In general, interactive read-alouds provide opportunities for students to share prior knowledge and experiences, interact with the text and concepts introduced therein, launch conversations about the topics introduced, construct meaning, make predictions,

Habitats in the U.S. Lesson Plans

and draw comparisons. You may wish to mark places within the texts to pause to ask for student experiences, predictions, or other ideas. Each reading experience should focus on an ongoing interaction between students and the text, including the following:

- Allow students to share personal stories throughout the reading
- Ask students to predict throughout the story
- Allow students to add new ideas from the book to the KWL chart and their STEM Research Notebooks
- Allow students to add new words from the book to the vocabulary chart and their STEM Research Notebooks

The materials list for each lesson includes the books for interactive read-alouds that you will use in that lesson. A list of suggested books for additional reading can be found at the end of this chapter (see p. 112).

COMMON MISCONCEPTIONS

Students will have various types of prior knowledge about the concepts introduced in this lesson. Table 4.3 outlines a common misconception students may have concerning these concepts. Because of the breadth of students' experiences, it is not possible to anticipate every misconception that students may bring as they approach this lesson. Incorrect or inaccurate prior understanding of concepts can influence student learning in the future, however, so it is important to be alert to misconceptions such as those presented in the table.

Table 4.3. Common Misconception About the Concepts in Lesson 1

Topic	Student Misconception	Explanation
Habitats	An animal's home is its habitat	An animal's home is part of its habitat and provides shelter but not does not provide all its basic needs The surrounding environment, which includes the animal's home, is its habitat

PREPARATION FOR LESSON 1

Review the Teacher Background Information, assemble the materials for the lesson, duplicate the student handouts, and preview the videos recommended in the Learning Components section below. Present students with their STEM Research Notebooks and explain how these will be used (see pp. 12–13). Templates for the

STEM Research Notebook are provided in Appendix A, and a rubric for observations, student participation, and STEM Research Notebook entries is provided in Appendix B.

In this lesson, students will have the opportunity to predict, observe, and explain properties of a habitat in the Wonder Worms investigation. You should check with your school's policy on having students handle live animals in the classroom. If students are not able to handle the earthworms, options for this activity are to have volunteers assist with the activity and handle the earthworms, or to conduct the activity as a whole class with only the teacher handling the earthworms and create a single earthworm habitat.

You should secure worms in advance; either red earthworms or night crawlers can be used. You should decide in advance what to do with the worms after students complete the activity (for example, place them in a flowerbed near the school or take them home with you to place in your own garden). You should collect and prepare clear two-liter bottles by cutting the top three inches off. You may wish to have samples of the worm habitats prepared to show students (see p. 55 for instructions). Worms may be obtained from a bait shop or from a variety of online distributors. After students have made their observations of the worms, you should be prepared to place all the worms into moist soil for the remainder of the class. Plan for an area in which you will release them (a garden or other appropriate habitat) after the class is over. Review the NSTA Position Statement on responsible use of live animals in the classroom at *www.nsta.org/about/positions/animals.aspx*.

Students will track the local weather throughout the module. Create or purchase a weather chart for class use that will accommodate your needs based on your local weather patterns. A sample of weather symbols is provided at the end of this lesson. You may also wish to have students track the weather conditions individually; a sample weather chart is provided at the end of this lesson. You should adjust the weather-tracking methods to your region and the time of year. For example, if you live in an area where the weather is consistently warm, you may wish to focus on daily weather patterns, such as the change in temperature over the day and changes in the amount of cloud cover each day. Alternatively, if you are using this module in a place and during a time period in which seasonal weather changes are occurring, you may wish to focus on weekly trends, such as the number of days with a high temperature over 70° each week.

You may wish to create a "weather window" as a cue to students to observe the weather and to help them focus their attention on weather conditions. To do this, create a cardboard frame with an opening that is about 16" x 20" and with a frame width of about three inches. You may decorate the frame with weather symbols (for example, cloud, sun, raindrop cutouts). Either secure the frame to a classroom window through which students will observe daily weather conditions or be prepared to manually

Habitats in the U.S. Lesson Plans

place the frame against the window and ask students to look through it as they make their daily weather observations.

STEM Research Notebook entry #2 provides a template for students to record vocabulary words. You may wish to use this template throughout the module for students to record definitions and illustrations of key vocabulary words as they are introduced. Alternatively, you may wish to make a class chart of vocabulary words and choose one or two of the words on the chart for each lesson and have students write and draw each word on a separate piece of paper to keep in their notebooks. The template provides space for definitions and illustrations of three words. If you plan to use the template and will introduce more than three vocabulary words in a lesson, you should make numerous copies of the template for each student.

Zoo displays are an excellent way to demonstrate animal habitats and how animals and plants live together and interact with their environment. You may wish to schedule a zoo field trip during this module as an opportunity for students to experience zoo displays and animal habitats firsthand.

LEARNING PLAN COMPONENTS
Introductory Activity/Engagement

Connection to the Challenge: Begin each day of this lesson by directing students' attention to the module challenge, the Zoo Habitat Challenge:

> A zoo nearby has asked for our help! The zoo wants to change the way its animals are displayed so that they are grouped by habitat. Right now, similar types of animals are grouped together (for example, all snakes are in one area and all bears are in one area). Instead, the zoo officials want to change the displays to group animals by their habitats and needs information about the habitats of animals in the United States. Our class has been challenged to create guides that provide this information to the zoo.

At the start of the lesson, ask students what they know and what they wonder about habitats in zoos, creating a KWL chart. Next, ask students for their ideas about what they will need to know to create guides for the zoo, creating a class list of students' ideas and adding these to the "want to know" section of the KWL chart. Each day thereafter, hold a brief class discussion of how students' learning in the previous days' lessons contributed to their ability to complete the challenge, and add students' responses to the "learned" section of the KWL chart.

Science and Social Studies Classes: Introduce the module by holding a class discussion about habitats. Create KWL chart to record students' ideas. Following agreed-on rules for discussions, launch the module by holding a class discussion about habitats, asking students these questions:

- What are habitats?
- Are there different types of habitats?
- What kinds of habitats are there?
- Are habitats the same everywhere?
- Where and when have you seen various habitats?

Then, have students explore habitats by watching a video about animal habitats such as "What is a Habitat?" at *www.youtube.com/watch?v=ZrSWYE37MJs*.

Students will create a STEM Research Notebook entry after watching the video. Track student responses about habitats on a KWL chart before and after watching the video.

STEM Research Notebook Entry #1

Have students draw and label pictures of two habitats in their STEM Research Notebooks.

Ask students what kinds of different habitats they think are located in the United States (for example deserts, oceans, forests), creating a class list. Ensure that students have, at minimum, included the following:

- grasslands
- forest
- desert
- ocean
- freshwater
- coastal
- urban areas

Help students locate areas where various habitats are located in the U.S. on a map (for example, grasslands in the Midwest, forests in the Northeast, deserts in the Southwest). Discuss why those areas are ideal locations for specific animals to live (for example climate, food supply). Hold a class discussion the similarities and differences between parts of the U.S. in relation to weather, climate, and the animals, plants, and people that live there.

Mathematics Connection: Introduce students to the weather chart that the class will maintain throughout the module. Ask students for their ideas about why understanding weather might be useful for learning about animal habitats (for example, knowing

4 Habitats in the U.S. Lesson Plans

what the weather conditions are like over time helps us to understand what animals and plants will live in an area). Introduce the term *environment* to students and emphasize to them that weather is an important part of the environment in which they live and in which plants live.

Beginning on Day 1, at the start of every class, students will observe and chart, graph, identify, describe, and analyze patterns of local weather to make connections among daily weather and local habitats. These observations will be made throughout the module to provide a basis for comparison about the weather conditions that reflect the climate differences in other areas of the U.S. Working as a class, students should observe and chart the following daily:

- descriptions of the weather (such as sunny, cloudy, rainy, and warm)
- numbers of sunny, windy, and rainy days in a month
- observations of the Sun and Moon and temperatures to describe patterns that can be predicted (for example, pattern analysis and predictions could include that it is usually cooler in the morning than in the afternoon; different months have different numbers of sunny days and cloudy days; the Sun and Moon appear to rise in one part of the sky, move across the sky, and set)

Each week, access a weather report for a different region of the U.S. and compare the weather report to your local weather. Emphasize to students that all areas will have some days that are colder or warmer than other or rainier or drier, but that if we look at the weather conditions in an area over a longer period of time (for example, six months or a year) we will learn something about the climate there (for example, the climate is hot and dry, or the weather changes from hot in the summer to cold in the winter).

ELA Connection: Through group discussion, students will utilize and develop speaking and listening skills throughout the module. In addition, students will utilize and develop their reading and writing skills through their STEM Research Notebook entries and will build vocabulary knowledge through class discussions and readings.

Begin a class vocabulary chart using pictures and words. Add vocabulary words to this chart throughout the module and refer to the chart during class discussions and as students create their STEM Research Notebook entries. This chart should be posted on the classroom wall throughout the module.

STEM Research Notebook Entry #2

(See Preparation for Lesson 1, p. 50 for options for vocabulary words)

Have students record vocabulary terms as they are introduced, and add definitions using words and/or pictures.

Activity/Investigation

Science and Social Studies Classes and ELA Connection: Explain to students that animals and plants all need things to live and that they get these things from their habitats. Ask students for their ideas about what living things need to survive, creating a class list of students' ideas. Introduce the idea that all living things have basic needs. Show students a video about living things' basic needs such as "What Living Things Need" at *https://www.youtube.com/watch?v=2xiAacSg4bI*. After watching the video, ask students what the basic needs they saw are, creating a class list. The class list of living things should include:

- food
- water
- air
- shelter
- space

Next, explore animal habitats and animal homes through an interactive read-aloud of *Animals at Home* by David Lock. Emphasize to students that animals' homes (for example, a bird's nest or a bear's cave) are part, but not all, of an animal's habitat. After the read-aloud, ask students to share their ideas about how the animals' basic needs were met in their habitats. Have students create a STEM Research Notebook entry about how animals' basic needs are met.

STEM Research Notebook Entry #3

Have students draw a picture of an animal in its habitat, including its five basic needs.

Wonder Worms Activity

Students will investigate worm habitats in the Wonder Worms investigation. To introduce the activity, ask students to share what they know about earthworms, recording students' ideas on a KWL chart. Next ask students what they wonder about worms, recording students' responses on the KWL chart. Then, conduct an interactive read-aloud of *Wiggling Worms at Work* by Wendy Pfeffer. After the read-aloud, ask students to share what they learned, recording students' responses on the KWL chart. Ask students specifically what they learned about worms' habitats.

Habitats in the U.S. Lesson Plans

Students will use the predict/observe/explain process to structure their work. Students will observe worms in four different simulated habitats during this activity:

- A box with a moist paper towel
- A box with a dry paper towel
- A clear plastic bottle with moist soil
- A clear plastic bottle with dry sand

Tell students that they will create four different types of conditions for worms and will observe how the worms behave in each. (You may wish to have samples of the four habitats prepared to show students.) First, however, they will predict how the worms will behave in the habitats. Have students share ideas about what sort of habitats worms live in naturally and how they behave. Track student responses on a predict/observe/explain (P.O.E.) chart, a three-column table with columns labeled "Predict," "Observe," and "Explain." Students will record their predictions in their STEM Research Notebooks.

Ask your students, "Do you see more worms on the sidewalk after a rainy day or after a sunny day?" Be sure to explain that worms need at least a little bit of water to "breathe" and so they like wet environments. Students will create four habitats each with different sets of conditions (habitats).

Ask students:

- Where will the worm be when placed in a box with a moist paper towel after ten minutes?
- Where will the worm be when placed in a box with a dry paper towel after ten minutes?
- Where will the worm be when placed in a clear plastic bottle with moist soil after ten minutes?
- Where will the worm be when placed in a clear plastic bottle with dry sand after ten minutes?

STEM Research Notebook Entry #4

Have students record their predictions about how the worms will behave in each of the four habitats.

The following is the procedure for the Wonder Worms investigations:

Students will create four habitats for their worms and make observations. Students will record their observations in a STEM Research Notebook entry, and you should also record students' responses on the P.O.E. chart.

Direct students to prepare boxes by placing a moist paper towel in the bottom of one of the boxes and a dry paper towel in the bottom of the other. and prepare the clear plastic bottles (put moist soil in one and dry sand in the other). Next, have students gently place a worm in each container for ten minutes. After ten minutes, have students make their observations.

Ask students to observe what their worms are doing in each container. Ask:

- Where was the worm in the box with a moist paper towel after ten minutes?
- Where was the worm in the box with a dry paper towel after ten minutes?
- Where was the worm in a clear plastic bottle with moist soil after ten minutes?
- Where was the worm in a clear plastic bottle with dry sand after ten minutes?

Record student responses on the P.O.E. chart. Students will record their observations in STEM Research Notebook Entry #5.

STEM Research Notebook Entry #5

Have students record their observations about where the worms were in each of the habitats.

After students have made their observations, place all the worms in one of the clear plastic bottles with moist soil for the remainder of the class. Release the worms into a garden or other appropriate habitat after the class is over.

Next, make a list of the habitats in the U.S. on the board (the list students created in the Introductory Activity/Engagement section of this lesson) and ask students to share their ideas about what kinds of habitats in the U.S. earthworms might live in. Guide students to understand that earthworms do not live in deserts or in oceans or in freshwater. Circle the habitats where earthworms might live. Introduce the idea that earthworms are useful for farming or gardening. Ask students to share their experiences with seeing farms and gardens in the local community. Ask students to name things that come from farms (for example, vegetables, fruit, cows). Ask students for their ideas about how earthworms can be helpful to farmers and gardeners, creating a class list. Introduce to students the idea that earthworms play important roles in making the soil suitable for growing plants because of the way they tunnel and move through the soil.

Habitats in the U.S. Lesson Plans

Explanation

Science and Social Studies Classes: Revisit students' predictions from the Wonder Worms activity and have students compare their predictions to their observations using the P.O.E. chart and their STEM Research Notebook entries. Next, ask students to explain why they think the worms behaved as they did and whether their predictions were accurate, close, or not accurate. Have students share their ideas and explanations with the whole class (document responses on the P.O.E. chart) and in their STEM Research Notebooks.

> **STEM Research Notebook Entry # 6**
>
> Have students record their explanations for the worms' behavior in the different conditions in their STEM Research Notebook, using words and/or pictures.

Mathematics Connection: Ask students if they have pets and, if so, what kinds of pets they have, creating a class list. As students name pets, ask students to stand up if they have that kind of pet. As a class, count the number of students who have that type of pet and write the number beside the name of the pet. Add the number of students reporting having each type of pet to the class list. Review the list with the class, asking students what is the pet that most students have and that least students have.

Next, ask students what their pets' habitat is like (for example, a cage or aquarium located within their home). Introduce to students the idea that the classroom could be a habitat for pets. Conduct an interactive read-aloud of *Guinea Pigs Add Up* by Margaret Cuyler.

Elaboration/Application of Knowledge

Science and Social Studies Classes and ELA Connection: Remind students of the module challenge, the Zoo Habitat Challenge. Tell students that they will develop a reference manual for a zoo official who wants to change the layout of the zoo to group animals by habitat. Explain to students that, at this zoo, animals are currently grouped by type (for example, all snakes and all bears are grouped together). In order to regroup displays by habitats, the zoo officials need information about habitats. Ask students what they learned in this lesson that will be helpful to them in creating the guide, creating a class list of students' ideas.

Assess student learning for this lesson by having students draw and label pictures of two habitats. Compare student pictures and have students identify the differences in the pictures.

Habitats in the U.S. Lesson Plans

Mathematics Connection: Provide each pair of students with a plastic shoebox-sized bin filled with beans or plastic beads and with about ten to 12 "worms" (plastic fishing worms or chenille stems) and a pair of large plastic tweezers. Roll a die and tell students that they should take that number of worms out of their bins. Write that number on the board, drawing pictures of the corresponding number of "worms" beside it. Next, have students return the "worms" to the bin and mix up the beans or beads and worms. Roll the die again and ask students if the new number is greater than, equal to, or less than the previous number. Repeat the procedure several times.

Evaluation/Assessment

Students may be assessed on the following performance tasks and other measures listed.

Performance Tasks

- Wonder Worms worm habitats
- Lesson Assessment

Other Measures (using assessment rubric in Appendix B):

- Teacher observations
- STEM Research Notebook entries
- Participation in teams during investigations

INTERNET RESOURCES
Habitat information

- *www.skyenimals.com/browse_habitat.cgi*
- *http://environment.nationalgeographic.com/environment/habitats/*

Earthworms

- *https://kids.nationalgeographic.com/animals/invertebrates/facts/earthworm*
- *www.sciencelearn.org.nz/resources/17-earthworm-adaptations*

Bureau of Labor Statistics' *Occupational Outlook Handbook*

- *www.bls.gov/ooh/home.htm*

Habitats in the U.S. Lesson Plans

Interactive read-alouds

- *www.readingrockets.org/article/repeated-interactive-read-alouds-preschool-and-kindergarten*
- *www.readwritethink.org/professional-development/strategy-guides/teacher-read-aloud-that-30799.html*

NSTA Position Statement on responsible use of live animals in the classroom

- *www.nsta.org/about/positions/animals.aspx*

"What is a Habitat?" video

- *www.youtube.com/watch?v=ZrSWYE37MJs*

"What Living Things Need" video

- *www.youtube.com/watch?v=2xiAacSg4bI*

Habitats in the U.S. Lesson Plans

SAMPLE WEATHER SYMBOLS FOR CLASS WEATHER CHART

Copyright material from Johnson, Walton & Peters-Burton (Eds.) 2024, *Habitats in the United States, Grade K*, Routledge

Habitats in the United States, Grade K

STUDENT HANDOUT

Copyright material from Johnson, Walton & Peters-Burton (Eds.) 2024, *Habitats in the United States, Grade K,* Routledge

Lesson Plan 2:
Let's Explore Our Local Habitat!

In this lesson, students will explore habitats in the school neighborhood. Students will explore key components of habitats as they relate to the needs of living things and will consider the importance of shelter for animals as they use the engineering design process (EDP) to design and create models of shelters for humans living in various conditions.

ESSENTIAL QUESTIONS

- What is the habitat like where we live?
- How do habitats meet the needs of animals?
- What are the weather and climate like where we live?
- What types of animals and plants live where we live?
- What time of year is it? How can you tell?

ESTABLISHED GOALS AND OBJECTIVES

At the conclusion of this lesson, students will be able to do the following:

- Identify the components of habitats as shelter, water, food, air, and space
- Identify properties of their local habitat
- Identify how the local habitat meets the needs of several types of animals and plants
- Identify the steps of the EDP
- Use the EDP to design and build a model of a shelter for human beings
- Evaluate the influence local habitats have on culture and society
- Use technology tools to gather data

TIME REQUIRED

Eight days (approximately 30 minutes each; see Tables 3.7–3.8, p. 35)

MATERIALS

Required Materials for Lesson 2

- STEM Research Notebooks
- Computer with internet access for viewing videos

Habitats in the U.S. Lesson Plans

- Books:
  - *Forests* by Cathryn Sill
  - *The Prairie that Nature Built* by Marybeth Lorbieki
  - *At Home in the Prairie* by National Geographic Learning
  - *In the Desert* by Michaela Weglinski (National Geographic Publishers)
  - *A Desert Habitat* by Bobbie Kalman
  - *Life in a Wetland* by Allan Fowler
  - *Wetlands* by Cathryn Sill
  - *Oceans* by Cathryn Sill
  - *Sea-Grass Beds* by Kimberley Jane Pryor
  - *Mountains* by Cathryn Sill
  - *The Burgess Seashore Book for Children* by Thornton W. Burgess
  - *The Great Graph Contest* by Loreen Leedy
  - *My Neighborhood: Places and Faces* by Lisa Bullard
- Chart paper
- Markers
- U.S. Map
- Pencils (one per student)
- Crayons for use in STEM Research Notebook entries (one set per student)

Additional Materials for Our Neighborhood Walking Tour

- Tablets or cameras for students to take pictures (optional) – one per two or three students
- Clipboards (one per student)

Additional Materials for Shelter Me Activity (one for each team of three or four students)

- Four pieces of cardboard or poster board (each approximately 8" x 10")
- Two pairs of scissors
- Five large craft sticks
- Ten small craft sticks
- Five plastic straws
- Ten uncooked spaghetti noodles or chenille stems
- Four pieces of construction paper

Habitats in the U.S. Lesson Plans

- Two glue sticks
- One roll of masking tape

Additional Materials for Mathematics Connection

- One piece of lined paper per student

SAFETY NOTES

1. Instruct students to be aware of and avoid poisonous plants and insects, any refuse, sharps (broken glass), and other hazards when they are outdoors.

2. Immediately wipe up any spilled water or soil on the floor to avoid a slip-and-fall hazard.

3. Have students wash hands with soap and water after activities are completed.

CONTENT STANDARDS AND KEY VOCABULARY

Table 4.4 lists the content standards from the *NGSS, CCSS, NAEYC,* and the *Framework for 21st Century Learning* that this lesson addresses, and Table 4.5 presents the key vocabulary. Vocabulary terms are provided for both teacher and student use. Teachers may choose to introduce some or all of the terms to students.

Table 4.4. Content Standards Addressed in STEM Road Map Module Lesson 2

NEXT GENERATION SCIENCE STANDARDS
PERFORMANCE OBJECTIVES   • K-LS1–1. Use observations to describe patterns of what plants and animals (including humans) need to survive   • K-ESS3–1. Use a model to represent the relationship between the needs of different plants and animals (including humans) and the places they live   • K-PS3–1. Make observations to determine the effect of sunlight on Earth's surface
DISCIPLINARY CORE IDEAS   **LS1.C.** *Organization for Matter and Energy Flow in Organisms*   • All animals need food in order to live and grow. They obtain their food from plants or from other animals. Plants need water and light to live and grow   **ESS3.A.** *Natural Resources*   • Living things need water, air, and resources from the land, and they live in places that have the things they need. Humans use natural resources for everything they do   **PS3.B.** *Conservation of Energy and Energy Transfer*   • Sunlight warms Earth's surface

Continued

Habitats in the United States, Grade K

Habitats in the U.S. Lesson Plans

Table 4.4. (*continued*)

CROSSCUTTING CONCEPTS

Patterns
- Patterns in the natural and human designed world can be observed and used as evidence

Systems and System Models
- Systems in the natural and designed world have parts that work together

Cause and Effect
- Events have causes that generate observable patterns

SCIENCE AND ENGINEERING PRACTICES

Analyzing and Interpreting Data
- Analyzing data in K-2 builds on prior experiences and progresses to collecting, recording, and sharing observations
- Use observations (firsthand or from media) to describe patterns in the natural world in order to answer scientific questions. (K-LS1–1)

Developing and Using Models
- Modeling in K-2 builds on prior experiences and progresses to include using and developing models (i.e., diagram, drawing, physical replica, diorama, dramatization, storyboard) that represent concrete events or design solutions
- Use a model to represent relationships in the natural world

Planning and Carrying Out Investigations
- Planning and carrying out investigations to answer questions or test solutions to problems in K-2 builds on prior experiences and progresses to simple investigations, based on fair tests, which provide data to support explanations or design solutions
- Make observations (firsthand or from media) to collect data that can be used to make comparisons

COMMON CORE STATE STANDARDS FOR MATHEMATICS

MATHEMATICAL PRACTICES
- MP1. Make sense of problems and persevere in solving them
- MP2. Reason abstractly and quantitatively
- MP3. Construct viable arguments and critique the reasoning of others
- MP4. Model with mathematics
- MP5. Use appropriate tools strategically
- MP6. Attend to precision
- MP7. Look for and make use of structure
- MP8. Look for and express regularity in repeated reasoning

MATHEMATICAL CONTENT
- K.CC.B.4. Understand the relationship between numbers and quantities; connect counting to cardinality

- K.CC.B.4a. When counting objects, say the number names in the standard order, pairing each object with one and only one number name and each number name with one and only one object
- K.CC.B.4b. Understand that the last number name said tells the number of objects counted. The number of objects is the same regardless of their arrangement or the order in which they were counted
- K.CC.B.4c. Understand that each successive number name refers to a quantity that is one larger
- K.CC.C.6. Identify whether the number of objects in one group is greater than, less than, or equal to the number of objects in another group, for example, by using matching and counting strategies
- K.CC.C.7. Compare two numbers between 1 and 10 presented as written numerals
- K.MD.A.1. Describe measurable attributes of objects, such as length or weight. Describe several measurable attributes of a single object
- K.MD.A.2. Directly compare two objects with a measurable attribute in common, to see which object has "more of"/"less of" the attribute, and describe the difference. For example, directly compare the heights of two children and describe one child as taller/shorter
- K.MD.B.3. Classify objects into given categories; count the numbers of objects in each category and sort the categories by count

COMMON CORE STATE STANDARDS FOR ENGLISH LANGUAGE ARTS

READING STANDARDS
- RI.K.1. With prompting and support, ask and answer questions about key details in a text
- RI.K.3. With prompting and support, describe the connection between two individuals, events, ideas, or pieces of information in a text

WRITING STANDARDS
- W.K.2. Use a combination of drawing, dictating, and writing to compose informative/explanatory texts in which they name what they are writing about and supply some information about the topic
- W.K.5. With guidance and support from adults, respond to questions and suggestions from peers and add details to strengthen writing as needed
- W.K.7. Participate in shared research and writing projects (for example, explore a number of books by a favorite author and express opinions about them)

SPEAKING AND LISTENING STANDARDS
- SL.K.1. Participate in collaborative conversations with diverse partners about *kindergarten topics and texts* with peers and adults in small and larger groups
- SL.K.3. Ask and answer questions in order to seek help, get information, or clarify something that is not understood
- SL.K.5. Add drawings or other visual displays to descriptions as desired to provide additional detail

Continued

Habitats in the U.S. Lesson Plans

Table 4.4. (*continued*)

NATIONAL ASSOCIATION FOR THE EDUCATION OF YOUNG CHILDREN STANDARDS

- 2.G.02. Children are provided with varied opportunities and materials to learn key content and principles of science
- 2.G.03. Children are provided with varied opportunities and materials that encourage them to use the five senses to observe, explore, and experiment with scientific phenomena
- 2.G.04. Children are provided with varied opportunities to use simple tools to observe objects and scientific phenomena
- 2.G.05. Children are provided with varied opportunities and materials to collect data and to represent and document their findings (for example, through drawing or graphing)
- 2.G.06. Children are provided with varied opportunities and materials that encourage them to think, questions, and reason about observed and inferred phenomena
- 2.G.07. Children are provided with varied opportunities and materials that encourage them to discuss scientific concepts in everyday conversation
- 2.G.08. Children are provided with varied opportunities and materials that help them learn and use scientific terminology and vocabulary associated with the content areas
- 2.H.02. All children have opportunities to access technology that they can use
- 2.H.03. Technology is used to extend learning within the classroom and integrate and enrich the curriculum

FRAMEWORK FOR 21ST CENTURY LEARNING

- Interdisciplinary themes
- Learning and Innovation Skills
- Information, Media and Technology Skills
- Life and Career Skills

Table 4.5. Key Vocabulary in Lesson 2

Key Vocabulary	Definition
community	a group of people who live in the same area
design	to create a plan for something that will be made
engineer	a person who designs and builds things
neighborhood	an area where people live
region	a part of our country that can be described by its location and that is different than other parts in some way
shelter	a place or a building that protects living things from weather and dangers

Habitats in the U.S. Lesson Plans

TEACHER BACKGROUND INFORMATION

In this lesson, students will begin to use the engineering design process (EDP) as they plan and construct shelters for humans (Shelter Me activity). Students will begin to gain an understanding of engineering as a profession through using the EDP.

Engineering

Students begin to gain an understanding of engineering as a profession in this lesson as they learn to use the engineering design process (EDP) to create a plan for their container garden. Students should understand that engineers are people who design and build products and systems in response to human needs. For an overview of the various types of engineering professions, see the following websites:

- *www.engineergirl.org/33/TryOnACareer*
- *www.nacme.org/types-of-engineering*
- *www.sciencekids.co.nz/sciencefacts/engineering/typesofengineeringjobs.htm*

Engineering Design Process (EDP)

Students should understand that engineers need to work in groups to accomplish their work, and that collaboration is important for designing solutions to problems. In this lesson and the next one, students will use the engineering design process (EDP), the same process that professional engineers use in their work. A graphic representation of the EDP is provided at the end of this lesson. You may wish to provide each student with a copy of the EDP graphic or enlarge it and post it in a prominent place in your classroom for student reference throughout the module. Be prepared to review each step of the EDP listed on the graphic with students and emphasize that the process is not a linear one—at any point in the process, they may need to return to a previous step. The steps of the process are as follows:

1. *Define.* Describe the problem you are trying to solve, identify what materials you are able to use, and how much time and help you have to solve the problem.

2. *Learn.* Brainstorm solutions and conduct research to learn about the problem you are trying to solve.

3. *Plan.* Plan your work, including making sketches and dividing tasks among team members if necessary.

4. *Try.* Build a device, create a system, or complete a product.

Habitats in the U.S. Lesson Plans

5   *Test.* Now, test your solution. This might be done by conducting a performance test, if you have created a device to accomplish a task, or by asking for feedback from others about their solutions to the same problem.

6   *Decide.* Based on what you found out during the Test phase, you can adjust your solution or make changes to your device.

After completing all six steps, students share their solutions or devices with others. This represents an additional opportunity to receive feedback and make additional modifications based on that feedback.

In this lesson, students work as a class to proceed through the first three steps of the EDP: Define, Learn, and Plan as they address the module challenge. The following are additional resources about the EDP:

- *www.sciencebuddies.org/engineering-design-process/engineering-design-compare-scientific-method.shtml*

- *www.pbslearningmedia.org/resource/phy03.sci.engin.design.desprocess/what-is-the-design-process*

Regions of the U.S.

Students will use a map in this lesson to identify what part of the U.S. they live in. The aim of this is to emphasize that different areas of the U.S. have different geographical characteristics (for example, mountains, grasslands, or coastline) and weather patterns that result in different types of animal habitats. An option is to introduce students to the regions of the U.S. According to the United States Fish and Wildlife Service, *(www.fws.gov/about/regions)* the U.S. has eight regions: Pacific, Southwest, Midwest, Southeast, Northeast, Mountain-Prairie, Pacific Northwest, and Alaska. Before you begin this lesson, identify the region where you live:

- Region 1 (Pacific Region) includes the states of Hawaii, Idaho, Oregon, and Washington, as well as Pacific Island Territories

- Region 2 (Southwest Region) includes the states of Arizona, New Mexico, Oklahoma, and Texas

- Region 3 (Midwest Region) encompasses the states of Illinois, Indiana, Iowa, Michigan, Minnesota, Missouri, Ohio, and Wisconsin

- Region 4 (Southeast Region) stretches across ten states—Alabama, Arkansas, Florida, Georgia, Kentucky, Louisiana, Mississippi, North Carolina, South Carolina, and Tennessee

- Region 5 (Northeast Region) covers the District of Columbia and 13 states—Connecticut, Delaware, Maine, Massachusetts, Maryland, New Jersey, New Hampshire, New York, Pennsylvania, Rhode Island, Vermont, Virginia, and West Virginia

- Region 6 (Mountain-Prairie Region) includes the states of Colorado, Kansas, Montana, Nebraska, North Dakota, South Dakota, Utah, and Wyoming

- Region 7 (Alaska Region) covers the state of Alaska, and it is the only FWS region to manage a single state

- Region 8 (Pacific Northwest Region) includes the states of California and Nevada and the part of Oregon that encompasses the Klamath River watershed.

For more information on the U.S. regions and maps, see the U.S. Geological Survey Regions webpage at *www.usgs.gov/science/regions*.

COMMON MISCONCEPTIONS

Students will have various types of prior knowledge about the concepts introduced in this lesson. Table 4.6 outlines some common misconceptions students may have concerning these concepts. Because of the breadth of students' experiences, it is not possible to anticipate every misconception that students may bring as they approach this lesson.

Incorrect or inaccurate prior understanding of concepts can influence student learning in the future, however, so it is important to be alert to misconceptions such as those presented in the table.

Table 4.6. Common Misconceptions About the Concepts in Lesson 2

Topic	Student Misconception	Explanation
Engineers and the engineering design process (EDP)	All engineers are people who drive trains	Railroad engineers are just one type of engineer. The engineers referred to in this module are people who use science, technology, and mathematics to build machines, products, and structures that meet people's needs

Continued

Habitats in the U.S. Lesson Plans

Table 4.6. (*continued*)

Topic	Student Misconception	Explanation
	Engineers use only science and mathematics to do their work	Engineers often use science and mathematics in their work, but they also use many other kinds of knowledge to solve problems and design products, such as how people use products, what people's needs are, and how the natural environment affects materials
	Engineers work alone to build things	Engineers often work in teams and use a process to solve problems. The process involves creative thinking, research, and planning, in addition to building and testing products
Living things and resources	Different kinds of organisms do not compete with each other for resources such as water	All living things need food, water, shelter, sunlight and air and compete with each other for these resources

PREPARATION FOR LESSON 2

Review the Teacher Background Information provided, assemble the materials for the lesson, and duplicate the EDP graphic attached at the end of this lesson if you wish to hand this out to students or enlarge it to post in the classroom.

In this lesson, students will identify where they live on a map (i.e., their home geographic region) and learn about what types of habitats are present in this area. If possible, identify a short video that highlights features of a habitat in your region to share with students. Examples of videos include:

- Forest: "Animals in the Forest" at *www.youtube.com/watch?v=YEG08_h6aT8 and* "Forest Habitat" *at www.youtube.com/watch?v=6oSUkCaGV18*

- Grassland or prairie: "Prairie Habitat" *at www.youtube.com/watch?v=99_PymrsiHA*

- Desert: "Amazing Ways to Live in the Desert" at *www.youtube.com/watch?v=gaZKEc59g1w* "Desert Animals and Plants" at *www.youtube.com/watch?v=DAs7lqce1cI*

Habitats in the U.S. Lesson Plans

- Ocean/Coastal: "Animals Ocean" at *www.youtube.com/watch?v=_YtofuJ-TL4* and "Habitats: Seashores" at *https://www.youtube.com/watch?v=iRoSEsJ4Wkw*

Students will explore habitats in the neighborhood surrounding the school in the Our Neighborhood Habitats investigation in this lesson. You should familiarize yourself with your school's policy on outdoors activities. If your school policies prohibit your leaving the school grounds, an option is to make a videorecorded tour of the neighborhood that the class can view together and limit students' firsthand exploration to the school property. In addition, you should check the weather forecast and make appropriate preparations (for example, having students wear hats, and/or carry umbrellas). A field trip to a zoo is an option for this lesson. Make appropriate preparations if you choose to incorporate a field trip.

Students will work in teams of three or four students and use the EDP to design and build a human shelter in the Shelter Me activity. You may wish to enlist the assistance of adult volunteers or older students to work with teams as they move through the steps of the EDP. You should prepare cards in advance listing the conditions for which teams will build their shelters (for example, "hot weather," "cold weather," "windy weather," "rainy weather"). Prepare student building kits using the materials listed in the Materials section. You should also prepare some simple means to test student designs (for instance, for the windy weather group, you may wish to have a blow dryer or fan to simulate wind, for rainy weather, you might sprinkle water over the shelter).

LEARNING PLAN COMPONENTS
Introductory Activity/Engagement

Connection to the Challenge: Begin each day of this lesson by directing students' attention to the module challenge, the Zoo Habitat Challenge:

A zoo nearby has asked for our help! The zoo wants to change the way its animals are displayed so that they are grouped by habitat. Right now, similar types of animals are grouped together (for example, all snakes are in one area and all bears are in one area). Instead, the zoo officials want to change the displays to group animals by their habitats and needs information about the habitats of animals in the United States. Our class has been challenged to create guides that provide this information to the zoo.

Hold a brief class discussion of how students' learning in the previous days' lessons contributed to their ability to complete the challenge. Add students' responses to the "learned" column of the KWL chart you began in Lesson 1's Connection to the Challenge section.

Habitats in the U.S. Lesson Plans

Science and Social Studies Classes and Mathematics and ELA Connections: Students should continue to chart and discuss patterns of local weather each day throughout the module to draw connections among weather patterns and their local habitat.

Ask student to share their ideas about what needs to be available in a habitat so that a living thing can survive there. Remind students of the basic needs of living things and guide students to understand that habitats must contain:

- shelter
- water
- food
- air
- space

Choose an animal that your students are familiar with and discuss how its habitat provides these things. For example, a white-tailed deer's habitat is the forest; deer find shelter under trees, water in creeks or streams, food from the plants in the forest, clean air to breathe, and the forest provides space for them to live and raise their young (you may wish to point out that when deer lack adequate space, they may enter roadways and other areas inhabited by humans).

Next, guide students in identifying where they live using a U.S. map (see Teacher Background section for more information on U.S. regions). Students will explore a major type of habitat in this area by viewing a video (see examples of videos in the Preparation for Lesson 2 section, pp. 70–71) and participating in an interactive read-aloud about a habitat that can be found in the part of the U.S. where you live (book suggestions listed below). Students will create a STEM Research Notebook entry after the video and read-aloud. You should also document student responses on a KWL chart.

After you have shown students where you live on the U.S. map, ask students to share what they know about the weather and geographic features of their state or region (for example, are there mountains or is it flat?; are there distinct weather differences in the seasons?; are there bodies of water?).

If you were able to identify a video that highlights characteristics of a habitat in the part of the U.S. where you live, share that with students. Then, conduct an interactive read-aloud of a book that features habitats related to the area where you live. Book choices associated with different regions include:

- Forest: *Forests* by Cathryn Sill
- Grassland or prairie: *The Prairie that Nature Built* by Marybeth Lorbieki; *At Home in the Prairie* by National Geographic Learning

Habitats in the U.S. Lesson Plans

- Desert: *In the Desert* by Michaela Weglinski; *A Desert Habitat* by Bobbie Kalman
- Freshwater: *Life in a Wetland* by Allan Fowler; *Wetlands* by Cathryn Sill
- Ocean: *Oceans* by Cathryn Sill; *Sea-Grass Beds* by Kimberley Jane Pryor
- Mountain: *Mountains* by Cathryn Sill
- Coastal areas: *The Burgess Seashore Book for Children* by Thornton W. Burgess

Next, ask students to share what they learned about habitats in your area of the U.S. Document student responses on a KWL chart and have students document their learning in a STEM Research Notebook entry.

STEM Research Notebook Entry #7

Have students document their what they learned about their home habitat in their STEM Research Notebooks after the video and/or interactive read-aloud, using words and/or pictures.

Activity/Investigation

Science and Social Studies Classes: Students will investigate habitats through two activities: the Our Neighborhood Habitat investigation (walking tour of the school neighborhood) and the Shelter Me activity (using the EDP to design a human shelter).

Our Neighborhood Habitat

As you prepare for the Our Neighborhood Habitat investigation, discuss the following questions with students, recording their responses on chart paper:

- Where do we live? (Locate on map and globe)
- What is the habitat like where we live?
- What is the weather and climate like where we live?
- What season is it? How can you tell?
- What types of animals and plants live where we live?

Students will complete STEM Research Notebook entries before and during the walking tour (students should take STEM Research Notebook entry #9 with them on the walking tour and complete the entry during and after the walk).

Habitats in the U.S. Lesson Plans

STEM Research Notebook Entry #8

Before taking the neighborhood tour, have students document their responses to the questions listed above in their STEM Research Notebooks, using words and/or pictures.

Take your students on a walking tour of the school neighborhood, looking for animals, plants, and noticing sounds, smells, and evidence of effects of the weather. You may wish to have students take pictures of the animals, plants, and habitats they observe. Students should take STEM Research Notebook entry #9 on clipboards with them to record their observations about the animals, plants, and habitats they observe.

STEM Research Notebook Entry #9

Have students document their observations during and after the neighborhood tour in their STEM Research Notebooks, using words and/or pictures.

When the class returns from the walking tour, ask students to name the plants and animals they saw on their walking tour. Record students' responses on chart paper. Next, write each of the basic needs of living things on a separate piece of chart paper. Point students' attention to one basic need at a time, asking them what they saw on their walk that could meet the basic need. Write students' responses on the chart paper.

Shelter Me

Introduce the Shelter Me activity by holding a class discussion about shelter, asking students for their idea about what the word *shelter* means. Guide students to understand that a shelter is a place that protects people or animals from the weather and from danger from other animals. Ask students what kind of shelter animals use (bird nests in trees, holes in the ground, beaver dams). Next, ask students what kind of shelters humans use (for example, houses). Tell students that they are going to build human shelters. Ask students to list the parts of human shelters they typically see (for example, roof, door, windows).

Introduce the idea that engineers are people who design and build things and that they go through a series of steps to do this. Introduce students to the steps of the EDP (see Teacher Background for more information).

Group students in teams of three or four. Have each team choose a card describing the conditions for the shelter they will build using the cards you prepared (see Preparation for Lesson 2, p. 72). Alternatively, you may wish to have all teams build a shelter for a single weather condition.

As a class, work through the Define and Learn steps of the EDP, recording students' responses on chart paper. For the Define step, ask students what the problem is that they are being asked to solve (build a shelter to protect people from weather). For the Learn step of the EDP, ask students what they think they need to know to complete this task (for example, what materials they can use, how much time they have). After completing these steps, show students the materials they will have to work with to build their shelters.

Tell students that during the Plan step of the EDP, each student will create a drawing of a structure they could build for the conditions they have been assigned (see STEM Research Notebook entry #10). Students should keep in mind the materials they have to work with as they create their drawings. After each student has drawn a picture, have team members compare their drawings and either choose one drawing or components of different students' drawings to use in their team's shelter design.

STEM Research Notebook Entry #10

Have students each create a drawing of a shelter they could create using the given materials in their STEM Research Notebooks. Students should label or be able to explain the materials they would use to build the model of this shelter.

Once students have completed their drawings and teams have chosen a design, give student teams their supplies and have students build their shelters (the Try step of the EDP). Remind students to refer to their drawing as they build their shelters.

You may wish to combine the Test, Decide, and Share steps of the EDP, having student teams present their designs to the class and conducting the test as a whole class. For the Test step, be prepared to simulate the given weather conditions (see Preparation for Lesson 2, p. 72). As a whole class, decide if the design is adequate to withstand the given weather conditions and what could be modified on the design to improve it.

Mathematics and ELA Connections: Show students the chart paper on which you tracked the findings from the Our Neighborhood Habitat investigation about the numbers of each kind of plant and animal students observed. Ask students to name the animal that was most observed and the plant that was most observed. Ask students how they know that these were the most frequently observed plants and animals. Ask students if they can think of any other ways to present this information that would make it easier to identify most, least, and equal. Introduce graphing through an interactive read-aloud of *The Great Graph Contest* by Loreen Leedy. After the read-aloud, ask students what they learned about how numbers can tell people about things. Next, ask students to name the different ways numbers were displayed in the book and how they could show the numbers of plants and animals they observed to help people understand what they found. As a class, create a bar graph to track the number and types of plants and animals students observed.

Habitats in the U.S. Lesson Plans

Explanation

Science and Social Studies Classes and ELA Connection: Conduct an interactive read-aloud about a habitat that is not common to the part of the U.S. where you live (see Materials list for this lesson, p. 62, for book choices). For example, if you live in the Midwest, you may wish to choose a reading about the desert or about coastal habitats. Prepare a t-chart with columns labeled "same" and "different." As a class, compare and contrast the habitat you read about with the local habitat students learned about.

Mathematics Connection: After students have completed their list comparing and contrasting the habitat they read about with the habitat found in the area where you live, ask students to identify whether there are more similarities or more differences. As a class, count the number of similarities students identified and record the number on the chart. Then, count the number of differences students identified and record that number on the chart. Ask students if the number of similarities is smaller than, the same as, or larger than, the number of differences. Once the class has come to a conclusion, record the relationship between the numbers on the board or on chart paper using the symbols <, =, or >.

Elaboration/Application of Knowledge

Science and Social Studies Class and ELA Connection: Create headers for each of the basic needs of animals on pieces of chart paper. Draw students' attention to one need at a time and ask students to name how their own basic needs are met (for example, food from the grocery store, shelter from a house or apartment). Introduce the word *community* to students and tell students that communities are groups of people who live close to one another and have their basic needs met in the same neighborhood, town, or city. This neighborhood, town, or city is a habitat for them. Conduct an interactive read-aloud of *My Neighborhood: Places and Faces* by Lisa Bullard. After the read-aloud, ask students to name the ways that people's needs were met in that neighborhood. Record students' responses on chart paper and have students complete a STEM Research Notebook entry.

> **STEM Research Notebook Entry #11**
>
> Have students record their ideas about how people's needs are met in communities in their STEM Research Notebooks, using words and/or pictures.

Assess student learning by having students draw and label a picture of one animal and one plant from their local habitat. Compare student pictures. Allow students to identify the differences in the pictures.

Mathematics Connection: Have students practice comparing numbers and expressing the relationships using <, =, and >. Show students two sets of items at a time (for example, pencils and crayons, large balls and small balls, toy cars and dolls) and ask them to count each set of items then write the relationship between the numbers on lined paper. Next, have students state the relationships as sentences, either orally or in writing (for example, the number of pencils is greater than the number of crayons, the number of large balls is less than the number of small balls, the number of toy cars is the same as the number of dolls).

Evaluation/Assessment

Students may be assessed on the following performance tasks and other measures listed.

Performance Tasks

- Our Neighborhood Habitats investigation
- Shelter Me structures
- Lesson Assessment

Other Measures (using assessment rubric in Appendix B)

- Teacher observations
- STEM Research Notebook entries
- Participation in teams during investigations

INTERNET RESOURCES
Engineering careers

- *www.engineergirl.org/33/TryOnACareer*
- *www.nacme.org/types-of-engineering*
- *www.sciencekids.co.nz/sciencefacts/engineering/typesofengineeringjobs.html*

Engineering design process

- *www.sciencebuddies.org/engineering-design-process/engineering-design-compare-scientific-method.shtml*
- *www.pbslearningmedia.org/resource/phy03.sci.engin.design.desprocess/what-is-the-design-process*

Habitats in the U.S. Lesson Plans

Regions of the U.S.
- *www.fws.gov/about/regions*
- *www.usgs.gov/science/regions*

Videos of Habitats
- "Animals in the Forest": *www.youtube.com/watch?v=YEG08_h6aT8*
- "Prairie Habitat" : *www.youtube.com/watch?v=99_PymrsiHA*
- "Amazing Ways to Live in the Desert": *www.youtube.com/watch?v=gaZKEc59g1w*
- "Animals Ocean": *www.youtube.com/watch?v=_YtofuJ-TL4*
- "Habitats: Seashores" at *https://www.youtube.com/watch?v=iRoSEsJ4Wkw*

ENGINEERING DESIGN PROCESS

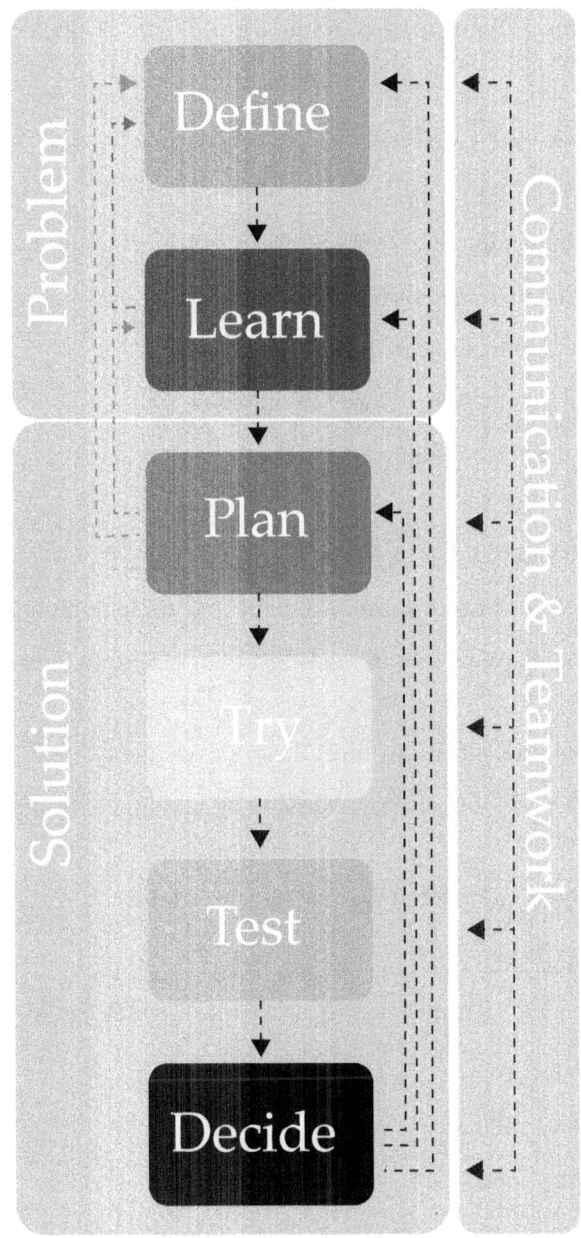

Copyright © 2015 PictureSTEM-Purdue University Research Foundation

4 Habitats in the U.S. Lesson Plans

Lesson Plan 3: Let's Explore Habitats throughout the United States!

In this lesson, students will explore habitats in the U.S. outside their home region. Students will use the EDP to create dioramas of U.S. habitats located in regions other than their own.

ESSENTIAL QUESTIONS

- What habitats are in the U.S.?
- What is the climate like where we live?
- What is the climate like in other parts of the U.S.?
- What types of animals live in other U.S. habitats?
- What types of plants live in other U.S. habitats?
- How do you think the climate affects the animals, plants, and people in other parts of the U.S.?

ESTABLISHED GOALS AND OBJECTIVES

At the conclusion of this lesson, students will be able to do the following:

- Identify several habitats within the U.S. and describe characteristics of those habitats
- Describe how various habitats meet the basic needs of animals and plants
- Use their understanding of characteristics of habitats to design and construct models of habitats
- Describe differences between various habitats in the U.S.

TIME REQUIRED

Six days (approximately 30 minutes each; see Tables 3.8–3.9, pp. 35–36).

MATERIALS

Required Materials for Lesson 3

- STEM Research Notebooks
- Computer with internet access for viewing videos

Habitats in the U.S. Lesson Plans

- Book choices associated with habitats in various regions of the U.S.:
    - *Forests* by Cathryn Sill
    - *The Prairie that Nature Built* by Marybeth Lorbieki
    - *At Home in the Prairie* by National Geographic Learning
    - *In the Desert* by Michaela Weglinski
    - *A Desert Habitat* by Bobbie Kalman
    - *Life in a Wetland* by Allan Fowler
    - *Wetlands* by Cathryn Sill
    - *Oceans* by Cathryn Sill
    - *Sea-Grass Beds* by Kimberley Jane Pryor
    - *Mountains* by Cathryn Sill
- Chart paper
- Markers
- U.S. map
- Pencils (one per student)
- Crayons for use in STEM Research Notebook entries (one set per student)

Additional Materials for My Dynamic Habitat Diorama investigation (one for each team of three or four students)

- Two cardboard or plastic shoeboxes for dioramas
- Three or four pairs of scissors
- Glue
- One set of markers
- One roll of clear tape
- Ten chenille stems (green, brown, and other various colors)
- Sheets of construction paper (blue, green, tan, brown, and other assorted colors)
- Optional: pictures of plants or small replicas of plants that will fit inside the shoebox

SAFETY NOTES

1. Students should use caution when handling scissors, as the sharp points and blades can cut or puncture skin.

4 Habitats in the U.S. Lesson Plans

CONTENT STANDARDS AND KEY VOCABULARY

Table 4.7 lists the content standards from the *NGSS, CCSS, NAEYC,* and the *Framework for 21st Century Learning* that this lesson addresses, and Table 4.8 (p. 85) presents the key vocabulary. Vocabulary terms are provided for both teacher and student use. Teachers may choose to introduce some or all of the terms to students.

Table 4.7. Content Standards Addressed in STEM Road Map Module Lesson 3

NEXT GENERATION SCIENCE STANDARDS

PERFORMANCE OBJECTIVES
- K-LS1–1. Use observations to describe patterns of what plants and animals (including humans) need to survive
- K-ESS3–1. Use a model to represent the relationship between the needs of different plants and animals (including humans) and the places they live
- K-PS3–1. Make observations to determine the effect of sunlight on Earth's surface

DISCIPLINARY CORE IDEAS

LS1.C. Organization for Matter and Energy Flow in Organisms
- All animals need food in order to live and grow. They obtain their food from plants or from other animals. Plants need water and light to live and grow

ESS3.A. Natural Resources
- Living things need water, air, and resources from the land, and they live in places that have the things they need. Humans use natural resources for everything they do

PS3.B. Conservation of Energy and Energy Transfer
- Sunlight warms Earth's surface

CROSSCUTTING CONCEPTS

Patterns
- Patterns in the natural and human designed world can be observed and used as evidence

Systems and System Models
- Systems in the natural and designed world have parts that work together

Cause and Effect
- Events have causes that generate observable patterns

SCIENCE AND ENGINEERING PRACTICES

Analyzing and Interpreting Data
- Analyzing data in K-2 builds on prior experiences and progresses to collecting, recording, and sharing observations
- Use observations (firsthand or from media) to describe patterns in the natural world in order to answer scientific questions (K-LS1–1)

Developing and Using Models
- Modeling in K-2 builds on prior experiences and progresses to include using and developing models (i.e., diagram, drawing, physical replica, diorama, dramatization, storyboard) that represent concrete events or design solutions
- Use a model to represent relationships in the natural world

COMMON CORE STATE STANDARDS FOR MATHEMATICS

MATHEMATICAL PRACTICES
- MP1. Make sense of problems and persevere in solving them
- MP2. Reason abstractly and quantitatively
- MP3. Construct viable arguments and critique the reasoning of others
- MP4. Model with mathematics
- MP5. Use appropriate tools strategically
- MP6. Attend to precision
- MP7. Look for and make use of structure
- MP8. Look for and express regularity in repeated reasoning

MATHEMATICAL CONTENT
- K.CC.B.4. Understand the relationship between numbers and quantities; connect counting to cardinality
- K.CC.B.4a. When counting objects, say the number names in the standard order, pairing each object with one and only one number name and each number name with one and only one object
- K.CC.B.4b. Understand that the last number name said tells the number of objects counted. The number of objects is the same regardless of their arrangement or the order in which they were counted
- K.CC.B.4c. Understand that each successive number name refers to a quantity that is one larger
- K.CC.C.6. Identify whether the number of objects in one group is greater than, less than, or equal to the number of objects in another group, for example, by using matching and counting strategies
- K.CC.C.7. Compare two numbers between 1 and 10 presented as written numerals
- K.MD.A.1. Describe measurable attributes of objects, such as length or weight. Describe several measurable attributes of a single object
- K.MD.A.2. Directly compare two objects with a measurable attribute in common, to see which object has "more of"/"less of" the attribute, and describe the difference. For example, directly compare the heights of two children and describe one child as taller/shorter
- K.MD.B.3. Classify objects into given categories; count the numbers of objects in each category and sort the categories by count

COMMON CORE STATE STANDARDS FOR ENGLISH LANGUAGE ARTS

READING STANDARDS
- RI.K.1. With prompting and support, ask and answer questions about key details in a text
- RI.K.3. With prompting and support, describe the connection between two individuals, events, ideas, or pieces of information in a text

Continued

Habitats in the U.S. Lesson Plans

Table 4.7. (*continued*)

WRITING STANDARDS
- W.K.2. Use a combination of drawing, dictating, and writing to compose informative/explanatory texts in which they name what they are writing about and supply some information about the topic
- W.K.5. With guidance and support from adults, respond to questions and suggestions from peers and add details to strengthen writing as needed
- W.K.7. Participate in shared research and writing projects (for example, explore a number of books by a favorite author and express opinions about them)

SPEAKING AND LISTENING STANDARDS
- SL.K.1. Participate in collaborative conversations with diverse partners about *kindergarten topics and texts* with peers and adults in small and larger groups
- SL.K.3. Ask and answer questions in order to seek help, get information, or clarify something that is not understood
- SL.K.5. Add drawings or other visual displays to descriptions as desired to provide additional detail

NATIONAL ASSOCIATION FOR THE EDUCATION OF YOUNG CHILDREN STANDARDS
- 2.G.02. Children are provided with varied opportunities and materials to learn key content and principles of science
- 2.G.03. Children are provided with varied opportunities and materials that encourage them to use the five senses to observe, explore, and experiment with scientific phenomena
- 2.G.04. Children are provided with varied opportunities to use simple tools to observe objects and scientific phenomena
- 2.G.05. Children are provided with varied opportunities and materials to collect data and to represent and document their findings (for example, through drawing or graphing)
- 2.G.06. Children are provided with varied opportunities and materials that encourage them to think, questions, and reason about observed and inferred phenomena
- 2.G.07. Children are provided with varied opportunities and materials that encourage them to discuss scientific concepts in everyday conversation
- 2.G.08. Children are provided with varied opportunities and materials that help them learn and use scientific terminology and vocabulary associated with the content areas
- 2.H.02. All children have opportunities to access technology that they can use
- 2.H.03. Technology is used to extend learning within the classroom and integrate and enrich the curriculum

FRAMEWORK FOR 21ST CENTURY LEARNING
- Interdisciplinary themes
- Learning and Innovation Skills
- Information, Media and Technology Skills
- Life and Career Skills

Habitats in the U.S. Lesson Plans

Table 4.8. Key Vocabulary in Lesson 3

Key Vocabulary	Definition
diorama	a three-dimensional model of a place or a scene

TEACHER BACKGROUND INFORMATION

Students will explore various habitats in the U.S. in this lesson. One means of providing students with experiences with other habitats is via webcams placed in nature sanctuaries and zoos. Examples of animal webcams include:

- *www.mangolinkcam.com/*
- *www.dceaglecam.org*
- *www.explore.org/livecams/spoonbills/alligator-spoonbill-swamp-cam*
- *www.montereybayaquarium.org/animals-and-exhibits/live-web-cams/sea-otter-cam*
- *http://web4.audubon.org/bird/puffin/PuffinCam.html*

Student teams will use the EDP to create models of habitats around the U.S. in the My Dynamic Habitat Diorama investigation. The information teams collect in this activity will be used for the reference manual they will create in the final module challenge.

COMMON MISCONCEPTIONS

Students will have various types of prior knowledge about the concepts introduced in this lesson. Table 4.9 outlines a common misconception students may have concerning

Table 4.9. Common Misconception About the Concepts in Lesson 3

Topic	Student Misconception	Explanation
Weather and climate	Weather and climate are the same	Climate refers to long-term weather patterns observed over many years; weather is the daily conditions in an area Observing the daily weather may not give us accurate information about the climate (for example, even though the desert is very dry, there may be rain on some days)

4 Habitats in the U.S. Lesson Plans

these concepts. Because of the breadth of students' experiences, it is not possible to anticipate every misconception that students may bring as they approach this lesson. Incorrect or inaccurate prior understanding of concepts can influence student learning in the future, however, so it is important to be alert to misconceptions such as those presented in the table.

PREPARATION FOR LESSON 3

Review the Teacher Background Information provided, assemble the materials for the lesson, and preview the videos recommended in the Learning Plan Components section below.

You should identify two habitats in two other areas of the U.S. for students to investigate during this lesson (see Lesson 2 Teacher Background, pp. 68–69, for a list of U.S. regions). You should choose habitats that are distinctly different from each other and from your own habitat. Be prepared to show students a video or videos that highlight these habitats. Examples of videos are provided in Preparation for Lesson 2 (pp. 70–71). You should also have on hand books to read out loud as a class about each of the habitats (see list of books for habitats in the Materials list, p. 81).

Student teams will create habitat dioramas that include two animals and two plants native to the habitat. You may wish to have students use textbooks or other reference books for this information. You should be prepared to direct students to this information. Alternatively, you may wish to use internet resources for this information; in this case, you should prepare information sheets for students in advance that includes basic information about each habitat as well as a list of plants and animals that are found in the habitats, with accompanying pictures. You may wish to plan to have volunteers on hand to assist groups that need extra support in creating their habitats.

Student teams will need shoeboxes to create dioramas. Have on hand enough cardboard or plastic shoeboxes to provide two for every three or four students in the class. An option for this activity is to have each team create just one diorama; in this case, you should assign each group one of the three habitats and each team will need only one shoebox.

LEARNING PLAN COMPONENTS
Introductory Activity/Engagement

Connection to the Challenge: Begin each day of this lesson by directing students' attention to the module challenge, the Zoo Habitat Challenge:

> A zoo nearby has asked for our help! The zoo wants to change the way its animals are displayed so that they are grouped by habitat. Right now, similar types

of animals are grouped together (for example, all snakes are in one area and all bears are in one area). Instead, the zoo officials want to change the displays to group animals by their habitats and needs information about the habitats of animals in the United States. Our class has been challenged to create guides that provide this information to the zoo.

Hold a brief class discussion of how students' learning in the previous days' lessons contributed to their ability to complete the challenge. Add students' responses to the "learned" column of the KWL chart you began in Lesson 1's Connection to the Challenge section.

Science and Social Studies Classes and Mathematics Connection: Students should continue to chart and discuss patterns of local weather each day throughout the module to draw connections among weather patterns and their local habitat.

Remind students that in the module challenge they will create a habitat reference manual for a zoo that wants to regroup its animal displays by habitat. Ask students if they think that knowing about their local habitat is enough to create this manual. Emphasize to students that zoos include animals from many different places. Tell students that for their challenge they have been asked to consider habitats all across the U.S., so in this lesson they will collect information about other habitats in the U.S. to include in their reference guides.

Introduce student to two habitats that are different from the local habitat students learned about and that are found in two different parts of the U.S. As a class, discuss what part of the U.S. these habitats might be found in and work as a class to locate those areas on a U.S. map. Next, hold a class discussion about what students know and wonder about these habitats, tracking student responses on a KWL chart.

Following agreed-on rules for discussions, ask your students (for each of the two alternative habitats):

- Where in the U.S. is the habitat found?
- What is the habitat like?
- What types of animals live in this habitat?
- What types of plants live in this habitat?
- How do you think the weather and climate affects the animals, plants, and people in that habitat?

Next, have students view a video about each of the habitats (see Preparation for Lesson 2, pp. 70–71). After viewing each video, ask students what they learned about the

4 Habitats in the U.S. Lesson Plans

habitat, tracking student responses on the KWL chart and having students record their ideas in a STEM Research Notebook entry.

STEM Research Notebook Entry #12

Have students document what they learned about each of the two habitats in their STEM Research Notebooks, using words and/or pictures.

Activity/Investigation

Science and Social Studies Classes and ELA Connection: Activities for this lesson will focus on the alternative habitats students are learning about. Student teams will create dioramas of the two habitats in the My Dynamic Habitat Diorama activity. You may either choose to have each team of students create a diorama for each of two habitats, or you may assign each team one of the three habitats (the home habitat or one of the two other habitats). Students will use the steps of the EDP process as they plan and build their dioramas. First, students will need to be able to identify the name of the habitat, the part of the U.S. in which the habitat is found, and to describe the climate in that habitat. Conduct an interactive read-aloud for each of the two habitats (see Materials list, p. 81). After each read-aloud, have students record the information they learned in a STEM Research Notebook entry.

STEM Research Notebook Entry #13

For each of the two habitats, have students record the name of the habitat and, using words and/or pictures, record the part of the U.S. in which the habitat is found, and describe the climate in that habitat in their STEM Research Notebooks.

STEM Research Notebook entry #14 guides students through the steps of the EDP. Each student should complete the STEM Research Notebook entry; however, students should work in teams of three or four to create the dioramas. Student teams should make decisions about the plants and animals to include in their dioramas before recording the information in their STEM Research Notebook entries. You should work through the steps of the EDP as a class, recording student responses on chart paper, and having students record their progress in the STEM Research Notebook entry.

Student teams must include two animals and two plants in their dioramas in addition to the name of the habitat and, if you introduced geographic regions to students, the region. You may wish to have students use textbooks or other reference books to find information and/or you may wish to access Internet resources for this information.

Additionally, you may wish to have students observe animals and habitats via webcams during the Learn phase of the EDP. Examples of animal webcams are provided in the Teacher Background section for this lesson (p. 85).

STEM Research Notebook Entry #14

Have students work through the steps of the EDP as they work in teams to create two dioramas of the alternative habitats (see Preparation for Lesson 3, p. 86 for an alternative approach to this activity). Each diorama should include two animals, two plants, and be labeled with the name of the habitat and, if you introduced geographic regions to students, the region.

When you reach the Plan phase, have a set of supplies available to show students. At the Try phase of the EDP for each diorama, have supplies available for each team. Remind student to look back to STEM Research Notebook entry #13 to find the name of the habitats they are studying and, if you introduced geographic regions, the region.

Mathematics Connection: As a class, review the weather chart. Ask students for their ideas about how this information could be recorded in a graph (for example, a bar graph for the number of sunny days, cloudy days, rainy days, or a line graph for the temperature for one week), referring to the types of graphs presented in the Lesson 2 interactive read-aloud of *The Great Graph Contest* by Loreen Leedy. Work together as a class to create one type of graph.

Explanation

Science and Social Studies Classes and ELA Connection: Have each student team share their dioramas with the class, explaining the information communicated by the dioramas. Before students share, introduce the concept of presentation skills. Ask students for their ideas about what they can do to make sure that they tell the class about the diorama in a way that other students can understand, creating a class list. Emphasize to students that they should speak loudly enough to be heard, that they should look at their audience, and that everyone from their team should have a turn to speak.

Mathematics Connection: As student teams present their dioramas, create a class list of the animals and plants that are included in each diorama. After the presentations are complete, work as a class to create bar graphs for the number of times each type of animal and each type of plant was included in a diorama.

Elaboration/Application of Knowledge

Science and Social Studies Classes and ELA Connection: Assess student learning by having students draw and label pictures of the two habitats you introduced in this lesson. Compare student pictures. Allow students to identify the differences in the pictures.

Mathematics Connections: Work as a class to create a type of graph using the weather chart data different than the graph created in the Activity/Investigation Mathematics Connection.

Habitats in the U.S. Lesson Plans

Evaluation/Assessment

Students may be assessed on the following performance tasks and other measures listed.

Performance Tasks

- My Dynamic Habitat Dioramas and presentations
- Lesson Assessment

Other Measures (using assessment rubric in Appendix B)

- Teacher observations
- STEM Research Notebook entries
- Participation in teams during investigations

INTERNET RESOURCES
Animal webcams

- *www.mangolinkcam.com/*
- *www.dceaglecam.org*
- *www.explore.org/livecams/spoonbills/alligator-spoonbill-swamp-cam*
- *www.montereybayaquarium.org/animals-and-exhibits/live-web-cams/sea-otter-cam*
- *http://web4.audubon.org/bird/puffin/PuffinCam.html*

Habitats in the U.S. Lesson Plans

Lesson Plan 4: The Zoo Habitat Challenge

In this lesson, student teams will develop a reference guide for a zoo to help them change the layout of zoo displays to groupings by habitat rather than by types of animals. The reference guide will describe two habitats in the United States and will highlight the similarities and differences in their climate, and the animals and plants that live there. Student teams will present their reference guides, with an invited guest serving as the "zoo official."

ESSENTIAL QUESTIONS

- Where are various habitats in the U.S. located?
- How are various habitats similar?
- How are various habitats different?

ESTABLISHED GOALS AND OBJECTIVES

At the conclusion of this lesson, students will be able to do the following:

- Synthesize their learning about habitats to develop a reference guide about habitats in the U.S.
- Compare and contrast various habitats in relation to animals, plants, and weather patterns
- Present the information in their reference manuals to an audience

TIME REQUIRED

Five days (approximately 30 minutes each; see Tables 3.10, p. 36)

MATERIALS
Required Materials for Lesson 2

- STEM Research Notebooks
- Computer with internet access for viewing videos
- Books:
   o *My Visit to the Zoo* by Aliki
   o *The Berenstain Bears' Moving Day* by Stan Berenstain
   o *On Our Nature Walk: Our First Talk About Our Impact on the Environment* by Jillian Roberts

Habitats in the U.S. Lesson Plans

- Reference manual template (attached at end of lesson)
- Chart paper
- Markers
- U.S. Map
- Pencils (one per student)
- Crayons for use in STEM Research Notebook entries (one set per student)
- Student dioramas from Lesson 3
- Index cards (optional) (one per habitat) to create descriptions of the "zoo displays"
- Materials to create zoo features (optional) such as construction paper, scissors, card stock or poster board, and markers

CONTENT STANDARDS AND KEY VOCABULARY

Table 4.10 lists the content standards from the *NGSS, CCSS, NAEYC*, and the *Framework for 21st Century Learning* that this lesson addresses, and Table 4.11 presents the key vocabulary. Vocabulary terms are provided for both teacher and student use. Teachers may choose to introduce some or all of the terms to students.

Table 4.10. Standards Addressed in STEM Road Map Module Lesson 4

NEXT GENERATION SCIENCE STANDARDS
PERFORMANCE OBJECTIVES   • K-LS1–1. Use observations to describe patterns of what plants and animals (including humans) need to survive   • K-ESS3–1. Use a model to represent the relationship between the needs of different plants and animals (including humans) and the places they live   • K-PS3–1. Make observations to determine the effect of sunlight on Earth's surface
DISCIPLINARY CORE IDEAS   **LS1.C.** *Organization for Matter and Energy Flow in Organisms*   • All animals need food in order to live and grow. They obtain their food from plants or from other animals. Plants need water and light to live and grow   **ESS3.A.** *Natural Resources*   • Living things need water, air, and resources from the land, and they live in places that have the things they need. Humans use natural resources for everything they do   **PS3.B.** *Conservation of Energy and Energy Transfer*   • Sunlight warms Earth's surface

CROSSCUTTING CONCEPTS

Patterns
- Patterns in the natural and human designed world can be observed and used as evidence

Systems and System Models
- Systems in the natural and designed world have parts that work together

Cause and Effect
- Events have causes that generate observable patterns

SCIENCE AND ENGINEERING PRACTICES

Analyzing and Interpreting Data
- Analyzing data in K-2 builds on prior experiences and progresses to collecting, recording, and sharing observations
- Use observations (firsthand or from media) to describe patterns in the natural world in order to answer scientific questions

Developing and Using Models
- Modeling in K-2 builds on prior experiences and progresses to include using and developing models (i.e., diagram, drawing, physical replica, diorama, dramatization, storyboard) that represent concrete events or design solutions
- Use a model to represent relationships in the natural world

COMMON CORE STATE STANDARDS FOR MATHEMATICS

MATHEMATICAL PRACTICES
- MP1. Make sense of problems and persevere in solving them
- MP2. Reason abstractly and quantitatively
- MP3. Construct viable arguments and critique the reasoning of others
- MP4. Model with mathematics
- MP5. Use appropriate tools strategically
- MP6. Attend to precision
- MP7. Look for and make use of structure
- MP8. Look for and express regularity in repeated reasoning

MATHEMATICAL CONTENT
- K.CC.B.4. Understand the relationship between numbers and quantities; connect counting to cardinality
- K.CC.B.4a. When counting objects, say the number names in the standard order, pairing each object with one and only one number name and each number name with one and only one object
- K.CC.B.4b. Understand that the last number name said tells the number of objects counted. The number of objects is the same regardless of their arrangement or the order in which they were counted
- K.CC.B.4c. Understand that each successive number name refers to a quantity that is one larger

Continued

Habitats in the U.S. Lesson Plans

Table 4.10. (*continued*)

- K.CC.C.6. Identify whether the number of objects in one group is greater than, less than, or equal to the number of objects in another group, for example, by using matching and counting strategies
- K.CC.C.7. Compare two numbers between 1 and 10 presented as written numerals
- K.MD.A.1. Describe measurable attributes of objects, such as length or weight. Describe several measurable attributes of a single object
- K.MD.A.2. Directly compare two objects with a measurable attribute in common, to see which object has "more of"/"less of" the attribute, and describe the difference. For example, directly compare the heights of two children and describe one child as taller/shorter
- K.MD.B.3. Classify objects into given categories; count the numbers of objects in each category and sort the categories by count

COMMON CORE STATE STANDARDS FOR ENGLISH LANGUAGE ARTS

READING STANDARDS
- RI.K.1. With prompting and support, ask and answer questions about key details in a text
- RI.K.3. With prompting and support, describe the connection between two individuals, events, ideas, or pieces of information in a text

WRITING STANDARDS
- W.K.2. Use a combination of drawing, dictating, and writing to compose informative/explanatory texts in which they name what they are writing about and supply some information about the topic
- W.K.5. With guidance and support from adults, respond to questions and suggestions from peers and add details to strengthen writing as needed
- W.K.7. Participate in shared research and writing projects (for example, explore a number of books by a favorite author and express opinions about them)

SPEAKING AND LISTENING STANDARDS
- SL.K.1. Participate in collaborative conversations with diverse partners about *kindergarten topics and texts* with peers and adults in small and larger groups
- SL.K.3. Ask and answer questions in order to seek help, get information, or clarify something that is not understood
- SL.K.5. Add drawings or other visual displays to descriptions as desired to provide additional detail

NATIONAL ASSOCIATION FOR THE EDUCATION OF YOUNG CHILDREN STANDARDS
- 2.G.02. Children are provided with varied opportunities and materials to learn key content and principles of science
- 2.G.03. Children are provided with varied opportunities and materials that encourage them to use the five senses to observe, explore, and experiment with scientific phenomena
- 2.G.04. Children are provided with varied opportunities to use simple tools to observe objects and scientific phenomena

- 2.G.05. Children are provided with varied opportunities and materials to collect data and to represent and document their findings (for example, through drawing or graphing)
- 2.G.06. Children are provided with varied opportunities and materials that encourage them to think, questions, and reason about observed and inferred phenomena
- 2.G.07. Children are provided with varied opportunities and materials that encourage them to discuss scientific concepts in everyday conversation
- 2.G.08. Children are provided with varied opportunities and materials that help them learn and use scientific terminology and vocabulary associated with the content areas
- 2.H.02. All children have opportunities to access technology that they can use
- 2.H.03. Technology is used to extend learning within the classroom and integrate and enrich the curriculum

FRAMEWORK FOR 21ST CENTURY LEARNING
- Interdisciplinary themes
- Learning and Innovation Skills
- Information, Media and Technology Skills
- Life and Career Skills

Table 4.11. Key Vocabulary in Lesson 4

Key Vocabulary	Definition
fictional	something that is not true but is, instead, imaginary
natural	describes something in the world that is not made by people
nature	parts of the world that are not made by people
reference guide	a written work that gives information about a specific topic that is used by people interested in that topic to learn or to tell them how to do something

TEACHER BACKGROUND INFORMATION

Students will address the module challenge during this lesson, creating their Habitat Reference Guides (see template at the end of this lesson). Students should include their home habitat and one of the other habitats they investigated in Lesson 2.

COMMON MISCONCEPTIONS

Since in this lesson students are synthesizing their learning from previous lessons to create compost systems, no new misconceptions are introduced. It will, however, be helpful to review the misconceptions introduced in Lessons 1–3 and be alert to ongoing misconceptions such as those presented there.

Habitats in the U.S. Lesson Plans

PREPARATION FOR LESSON 4

Review the Teacher Background Information provided, assemble the materials for the lesson, and duplicate copies of the Habitat Reference Guide template for each student. Students will use their previous STEM Research Notebook entries to complete the guides, so they should have easy access to these. In addition, students will include pictures in their guides. You may either have students draw the pictures or you may wish to copy various images of habitats for students to glue into their reference guides.

After students have created their guides, teams will present their work to an audience of invited guests who will act as "zoo officials." You may wish to invite parents, school administrators, or representatives from an area zoo or nature center. Provide these guests with an overview of the project and provide samples of developmentally appropriate questions and comments. Students will use their dioramas from Lesson 3 to create a class "zoo." Prepare to have dioramas on hand and prepare additional images of habitats for students' use during their presentations.

LEARNING PLAN COMPONENTS
Introductory Activity/Engagement

Connection to the Challenge: Begin each day of this lesson by directing students' attention to the module challenge, the Zoo Habitat Challenge:

> A zoo nearby has asked for our help! The zoo wants to change the way its animals are displayed so that they are grouped by habitat. Right now, similar types of animals are grouped together (for example, all snakes are in one area and all bears are in one area). Instead, the zoo officials want to change the displays to group animals by their habitats and needs information about the habitats of animals in the United States. Our class has been challenged to create guides that provide this information to the zoo.

On the first day of the lesson, hold a brief class discussion of how students' learning in the previous days' lessons contributed to their ability to complete the challenge. Add students' responses to the "learned" column of the KWL chart you began in Lesson 1's Connection to the Challenge section. Each day thereafter, review students' progress on the challenge, and ask students to share challenges they are encountering. As a class, brainstorm ideas about how to overcome these challenges.

Science and Social Studies Classes and Mathematics and ELA Connections: Students should continue to chart and discuss patterns of local weather each day throughout the module to draw connections among weather patterns and their local habitat.

Habitats in the U.S. Lesson Plans

Hold a class discussion about zoos. Ask students if they have ever visited a zoo. Allow students to share their experiences, asking questions such as:

- What kinds of areas did the animals live in (i.e., cages, open areas)?

- How were the animals grouped (i.e., same kinds of animals all together, grouped by where they live in nature)?

- What did the zoo do to make the animals' living spaces like their natural habitats?

Record students responses on a KWL chart and ask them to add what they wonder about zoos that would be helpful to know for solving their challenge.

Next, conduct an interactive read-aloud of *My Visit to the Zoo* by Aliki. After the read-aloud, hold a class discussion about students' observations, and ask the questions listed above again, adding students' responses to the KWL chart.

Point out to students that there are different ways that zoos can group animal displays (for example, by area of the world where the animals live in nature, by type of animal). Remind students of the module challenge and tell them that they are working with a fictional zoo that currently has animals grouped by type of animal. This zoo wants to regroup its animals so that animals in the same or similar habitats are grouped together. To do this, the zoo needs information about various habitats and the living things in those habitats. Tell students that they are going to develop reference guides that will tell the zoo officials about two different habitats in the U.S. This guide will show the similarities and differences in the habitats in terms of the climate and animals and plants that live there.

Activity/Investigation

Science and Social Studies Classes and ELA Connection: Student teams should each decide on the habitats they will describe in their reference guides (their home habitat and one other). Then, using their learning from the module and their previous STEM Research notebook entries, students should complete the Habitat Reference Guide template. Guide students through each item in the template, and allow students to add extra pages on which they draw pictures or glue pictures you prepared in advance. Students are prompted to describe the climate by describing the weather during the winter and during the summer. You may wish to provide a word bank for students to choose from (for example: warm, hot, cold, cool, rainy, snowy, dry).

Mathematics Connection: Not applicable.

Habitats in the U.S. Lesson Plans

Explanation

Science and Social Studies Classes and ELA Connection: Remind students that they will present their Habitat Reference Guides to an audience of "zoo officials." Review good presentation skills with students (for example, allowing each person on the team a chance to speak; speaking one at a time; speaking in a clear, audible voice; looking at the audience). Each student completed his or her own reference guide; however, teams should make their presentations as a unit. Each student should therefore be assigned components of the guide to present and should use their own reference guide for that portion of the presentation.

Ask students to share their ideas about how people might live differently in different places in the U.S. (for example, in some places, they need to have heavy coats for winter, in others, they do not need cold weather clothing; in some places, they can go to the beach easily since it is close by; in others, they need to travel a long way to go to the beach), creating a list of students' ideas.

Conduct an interactive read-aloud of *The Berenstain Bears' Moving Day* by Stan Berenstain. Ask students to share their ideas about how moving to a new area (from the mountains to a tree house) changed everyday life for the characters in the book.

Next, ask students if plants and animals can change parts of the environment. You may wish to take a class vote and record the number of students who answer "yes" and the number who answer "no." Ask students who answered "yes" to explain why they answered this way and students who answered "no" to explain their responses. Ask students to recall some of the animals and plants they saw on their neighborhood walking tour in Lesson 1 and ask if any of these created changes in the environment (for example, students may have observed birds' nests in trees or cracks in sidewalks caused by tree roots). Introduce the idea to students that as living things live in a habitat, they do things that cause changes to the environment in order to have their basic needs met. Ask students to brainstorm ideas of how animals might change the environment (for example, squirrels burying nuts, bees building hives, spiders building webs, woodpeckers making holes in trees, rabbits digging burrows, birds dropping seeds that grow into plants, beavers making dams). Next, ask students to brainstorm ideas of how plants change the environment (nuts falling from trees or seeds falling from plants create new trees or plants, trees provide shade, trees and other plants provide homes for animals, tree roots push up through the ground and make a smooth area bumpy).

You may wish to have students view a video of how animals change the environment (for example, "Giant Gopher Digging a Hole" at *www.youtube.com/watch?v=_SwAVRg-GR0s*) and a video of how plants change the environment (for example, "Bean Time Lapse" at *www.youtube.com/watch?v=w77zPAtVTuI*). Hold a class discussion about what basic need was being met by the animals and plants (for example, shelter, space, food).

Habitats in the U.S. Lesson Plans

Ask students whether they think that people change their environments. Create a list of class ideas about how people impact their environment (for example, building houses and buildings, building roads, planting trees and flowers, making trash that has to be taken to a landfill). Conduct an interactive read-aloud of *On Our Nature Walk: Our First Talk About Our Impact on the Environment* by Jillian Roberts. Hold a class discussion of how people impacted the environment in the book and whether this impact was helpful or harmful to our habitat. Record the impacts on a class chart and then discuss whether students think each impact is helpful or harmful to people's habitat and to the habitat of other animals and plants. Ask students for their ideas about what people can do to make their impact less harmful and create a class list of these ideas.

Mathematics Connection: Not applicable.

Elaboration/Application of Knowledge

Science and Social Studies Classes and ELA Connection: Have student teams each present their Habitat Reference Guides to the invited guests and answer questions from other students and from the invited guests about their presentations. Students should emphasize similarities and differences in the habitats in terms of climate, and the animals and plants that live in those habitats.

Work as a class to create a "zoo" using students' dioramas, grouping like habitats together. You may wish to create brief descriptions of habitats on note cards using students' oral descriptions of the habitats they created. An additional option is to have students create other features of the zoo. For example, students could use construction paper to create paths between habitat areas, an entrance area, and other features.

Evaluation/Assessment

Students may be assessed on the following performance tasks and other measures listed.

Performance Tasks

- Habitat Reference Guides
- Team presentations to "zoo officials"

Other Measures (using assessment rubric in Appendix B)

- Teacher observations.
- Participation in teams during investigations.

4 Habitats in the U.S. Lesson Plans

INTERNET REFERENCES

"Giant Gopher Digging a Hole": *www.youtube.com/watch?v=_SwAVRgGR0s*

"Bean Time Lapse": *www.youtube.com/watch?v=w77zPAtVTuI*

Habitats in the U.S. Lesson Plans

Habitat Reference Guide

Name:
_____

_____

Habitats in the U.S. Lesson Plans

HABITATS

Identify your local habitat:

_____

_____

Color the part of the United States where your local habitat is located:

Copyright material from Johnson, Walton & Peters-Burton (Eds.) 2024, *Habitats in the United States, Grade K*, Routledge

Habitats in the U.S. Lesson Plans

Identify one other habitat in the U.S.:
_____

_____

Color the part of the United States where your local habitat is located:

4 Habitats in the U.S. Lesson Plans

Climate in your home habitat

What is the climate of your local habitat like?
_____
_____
_____

Habitats in the U.S. Lesson Plans 4

Draw a picture of the climate in the other habitat:

What is the climate like in the other habitat?
_____

_____

Copyright material from Johnson, Walton & Peters-Burton (Eds.) 2024, *Habitats in the United States, Grade K,* Routledge

Habitats in the United States, Grade K

Habitats in the U.S. Lesson Plans

Animals in Your Home Habitat

Write the name of and draw two animals that live in your local habitat:

1

Habitats in the U.S. Lesson Plans

2
_____

_____

Habitats in the U.S. Lesson Plans

Animals in Another Habitat

Write the name of and draw two animals that live in the other habitat:

1

2

Habitats in the U.S. Lesson Plans

Plants in Your Home Habitat

Draw three types of plants that live in your local habitat and write the names of the plants:

1.

2.

3.

Copyright material from Johnson, Walton & Peters-Burton (Eds.) 2024, *Habitats in the United States, Grade K,* Routledge

Plants in Your Home Habitat

Draw three types of plants that live in the other habitat and write the names of the plants:

1.

2.

3.

Habitats in the U.S. Lesson Plans

SUGGESTED BOOKS

Butterfield, M. 1999. *This Is a Watery Place. It Is Deep and Dark. Where Am I?* Thameside Press.

Chesanow, N. 1995. *Where do I Live?* B.E.S. Publishing.

Evans, S. 2018. *Animal Homes*. National Geographic Publishers.

Fowler, A. 1998. *Life in a Wetland*. Children's Press.

Gibbons, G. 2001. *Polar Bears*. Holiday House Press.

Gibbons, G. 1991. *Zoo*. HarperCollins.

Greve, M. 2009. *North, South, East, and West*. Rourke Educational Media.

Guiberson, B. 1993. *Cactus Hotel*. Square Fish Publisher.

Hyde, N. 2009. *Desert Extremes*. Crabtree Publishing Company.

Miche, M. 2012. *Nature's Patchwork Quilt: Understanding Habitats*. Dawn Publications.

Peterson, C. 2022. *A Trip to the Zoo with Sesame Street*. Lerner Publications.

Pryor, K. 2007. *Wonders of the Sea: Sea-Grass Beds*. Smart Apple Media.

Rockwell, A. 2018. *Zoo Day*. Aladdin.

Schifini, A. 2003. *Me on the Map*. National Geographic Publishers.

Sis, P. 2004. *The Train of States*. Greenwillow Books.

Szymanski, J. 2018. *In the Ocean*. National Geographic Publishers.

Wallace, K. 2018. *A Trip to the Zoo*. DK Publishers.

REFERENCES

Koehler, C., M. A. Bloom, and A. R. Milner. 2015. The STEM Road Map for grades K–2. In *STEM Road Map: A framework for integrated STEM education*, eds. C. C. Johnson, E. E. Peters-Burton, and T. J. Moore, 41–67. New York: Routledge. *www.routledge.com/products/9781138804234*.

TRANSFORMING LEARNING WITH HABITATS IN THE U.S. AND THE *STEM ROAD MAP CURRICULUM SERIES*

Carla C. Johnson

This chapter serves as a conclusion to the Habitats in the U.S. integrated STEM curriculum module, but it is just the beginning of the transformation of your classroom that is possible through use of the *STEM Road Map Curriculum Series*. In this book, many key resources have been provided to make learning meaningful for your students through integration of science, technology, engineering, and mathematics, as well as social studies and English language arts, into powerful problem- and project-based instruction. First, the Habitats in the U.S. curriculum is grounded in the latest theory of learning for students in grade K specifically. Second, as your students work through this module, they engage in using the engineering design process (EDP) and build prototypes in the same way engineers and STEM professionals do in the real world. Third, students acquire important knowledge and skills grounded in national academic standards in mathematics, English language arts, science, and 21st century skills that will enable their learning to be deeper, retained longer, and applied throughout, illustrating the critical connections within and across disciplines. Finally, authentic formative assessments, including strategies for differentiation and addressing misconceptions, are embedded within the curriculum activities.

The Habitats in the U.S. curriculum in the Sustainable Systems STEM Road Map theme can be used in single-content classrooms (for example, mathematics) where there is only one teacher or expanded to include multiple teachers and content areas across classrooms. Through the exploration of the Habitats in the U.S. lesson plans, students engage in a real-world STEM problem on the first day of instruction and gather necessary knowledge and skills along the way in the context of solving the problem.

Transforming Learning with Habitats in the U.S. and the *STEM Road Map Curriculum Series*

The other topics in the *STEM Road Map Curriculum Series* are designed in a similar manner, and NSTA Press and Routledge have published additional volumes in this series for this and other grade levels, and have plans to publish more.

For an up-to-date list of volumes in the series, please visit https://www.routledge.com/STEM-Road-Map-Curriculum-Series/book-series/SRM (for titles co-published by Routledge and NSTA Press), or https://www.nsta.org/book-series/stem-road-map-curriculum (for titles published by NSTA Press).

If you are interested in professional development opportunities focused on the STEM Road Map specifically or integrated STEM or STEM programs and schools overall, contact the lead editor of this project, Dr. Carla C. Johnson, Professor of Science Education at NC State University. Someone from the team will be in touch to design a program that will meet your individual, school, or district needs.

APPENDIX A
STEM RESEARCH NOTEBOOK TEMPLATES

APPENDIX A

MY STEM RESEARCH NOTEBOOK

HABITATS IN THE UNITED STATES

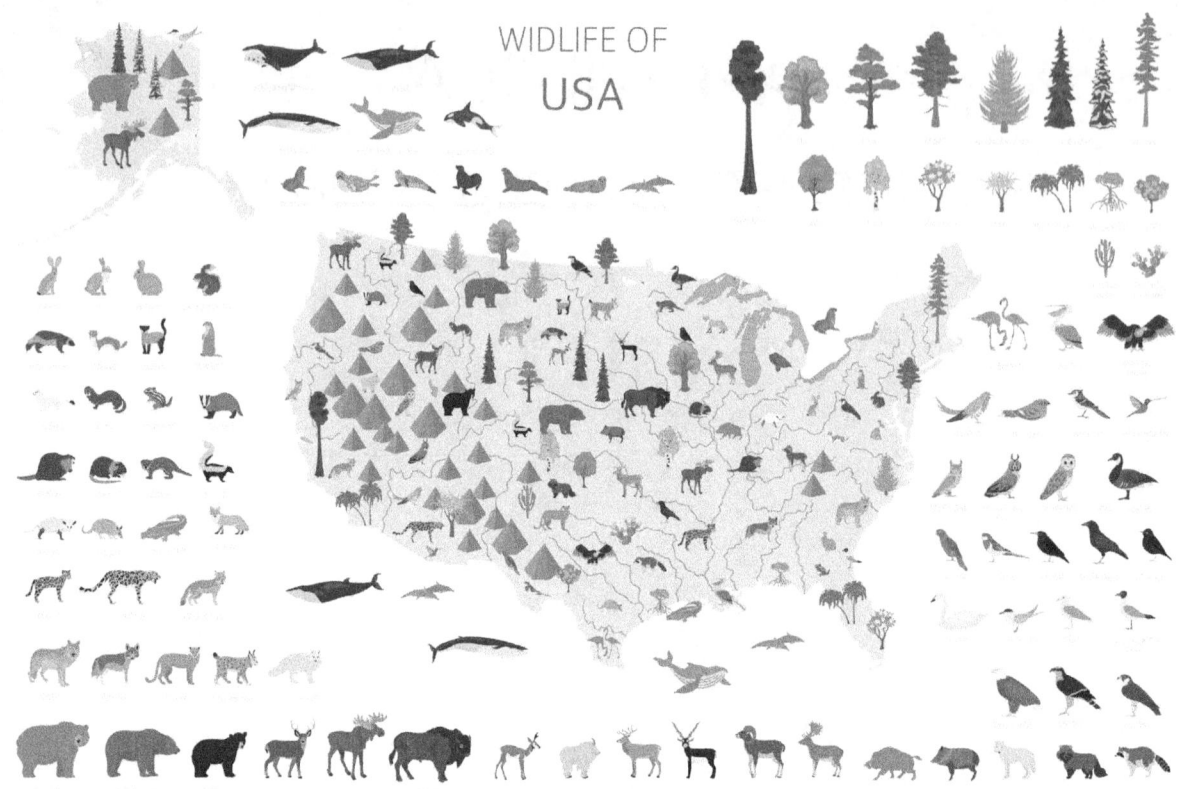

NAME
_____

_____

APPENDIX A

STEM RESEARCH NOTEBOOK #1 (LESSON PLAN 1)

NAME_____DATE_____

Draw and label two different habitats you have seen in person or in pictures

Copyright material from Johnson, Walton & Peters-Burton (Eds.) 2024, *Habitats in the United States, Grade K*, Routledge

APPENDIX A

STEM RESEARCH NOTEBOOK #3 (LESSON PLAN 1)

NAME_____ DATE_____

Vocabulary words

Word	Definition	Illustration

Copyright material from Johnson, Walton & Peters-Burton (Eds.) 2024, *Habitats in the United States, Grade K*, Routledge

APPENDIX A

STEM RESEARCH NOTEBOOK #3 (LESSON PLAN 1)

NAME_____DATE_____

Draw an animal and its habitat and show how its basic needs are met

Copyright material from Johnson, Walton & Peters-Burton (Eds.) 2024, *Habitats in the United States, Grade K*, Routledge

APPENDIX A

STEM RESEARCH NOTEBOOK #4, #5, AND #6 (LESSON PLAN 1)

NAME_____DATE_____

Wonder Worms

Circle or write in your predictions. Then, circle or write in your observations. Finally, write explanations (cause and effect)

QUESTIONS	PREDICTIONS	OBSERVATIONS	EXPLANATION
Where will the worm be after ten minutes when placed in a box with a moist paper towel?	On top of the towel Under the towel Next to the towel/On the side of the towel _____	On top of the towel Under the towel Next to the towel/On the side of the towel _____	
Where will the worm be after ten minutes when placed in a box with a dry paper towel?	On top of the towel Under the towel Next to the towel/On the side of the towel _____	On top of the towel Under the towel Next to the towel/On the side of the towel _____	
Where will the worm be after ten minutes when placed in a clear plastic bottle with moist soil?	On top of the soil Under the soil Next to the soil/On the side of the soil _____	On top of the soil Under the soil Next to the soil/On the side of the soil _____	
Where will the worm be after ten minutes when placed in a clear plastic bottle with dry sand?	On top of the soil Under the soil Next to the soil/On the side of the soil _____	On top of the soil Under the soil Next to the soil/On the side of the soil _____	

Copyright material from Johnson, Walton & Peters-Burton (Eds.) 2024, *Habitats in the United States, Grade K,* Routledge

APPENDIX A

STEM RESEARCH NOTEBOOK #7 (LESSON PLAN 2)

NAME_____DATE_____

I learned . . .
_____
- -
_____

Copyright material from Johnson, Walton & Peters-Burton (Eds.) 2024, *Habitats in the United States, Grade K*, Routledge

APPENDIX A

STEM RESEARCH NOTEBOOK #8 (LESSON PLAN 2)

NAME_____DATE_____

Our Neighborhood Habitat

- Where do we live? (city and state)

_____
_____
_____
_____
_____

Color the state where we live

Copyright material from Johnson, Walton & Peters-Burton (Eds.) 2024, *Habitats in the United States, Grade K*, Routledge

APPENDIX A

STEM RESEARCH NOTEBOOK #8, PAGE 2 (LESSON PLAN 2)

NAME_____DATE_____

- **What is the habitat like where we live? (for example, forest, prairie, desert, coastal)**

_____

_____

Draw a picture of the habitat where we live

Copyright material from Johnson, Walton & Peters-Burton (Eds.) 2024, *Habitats in the United States, Grade K*, Routledge

APPENDIX A

STEM RESEARCH NOTEBOOK #8, PAGE 3 (LESSON PLAN 2)

NAME_____DATE_____

Draw a picture of the weather today where we live

- What time of year is it? How can you tell?

_____

_____
_____

_____

Copyright material from Johnson, Walton & Peters-Burton (Eds.) 2024, *Habitats in the United States, Grade K,* Routledge

APPENDIX A

STEM RESEARCH NOTEBOOK #9 (LESSON PLAN 2)

NAME_____DATE_____

Our Neighborhood Habitat

Draw and label two animals you saw

Copyright material from Johnson, Walton & Peters-Burton (Eds.) 2024, *Habitats in the United States, Grade K,* Routledge

APPENDIX A

STEM RESEARCH NOTEBOOK #9, PAGE 2 (LESSON PLAN 2)

NAME_____DATE_____

Draw and label two plants you saw

APPENDIX A

STEM RESEARCH NOTEBOOK #9, PAGE 3 (LESSON PLAN 2)

NAME_____DATE_____

Draw and label two animals you heard

APPENDIX A

STEM RESEARCH NOTEBOOK #9, PAGE 4 (LESSON PLAN 2)

NAME_____DATE_____

Draw and label two things you smelled

Copyright material from Johnson, Walton & Peters-Burton (Eds.) 2024, *Habitats in the United States, Grade K,* Routledge

APPENDIX A

STEM RESEARCH NOTEBOOK #9, PAGE 5 (LESSON PLAN 2)

NAME_____DATE_____

Draw and label two ways you saw in which weather affects animals, plants, and people

Copyright material from Johnson, Walton & Peters-Burton (Eds.) 2024, *Habitats in the United States, Grade K*, Routledge

APPENDIX A

STEM RESEARCH NOTEBOOK #10 (LESSON PLAN 2)

NAME_____DATE_____

Shelter Me

Draw a picture of a shelter you could build to protect people from weather using the materials your teacher shows you

APPENDIX A

STEM RESEARCH NOTEBOOK #11 (LESSON PLAN 2)

NAME_____DATE_____

People's Needs Are Met in a Community

Show how each one of people's needs is met in a community

Food

Water

Shelter

Air

Space

Copyright material from Johnson, Walton & Peters-Burton (Eds.) 2024, *Habitats in the United States, Grade K*, Routledge

APPENDIX A

STEM RESEARCH NOTEBOOK #12 (LESSON PLAN 2)

NAME_____ DATE_____

The first habitat I learned about is

_____
_____
_____

I learned . . .

_____
_____
_____
_____
_____
_____
_____
_____

Copyright material from Johnson, Walton & Peters-Burton (Eds.) 2024, *Habitats in the United States, Grade K,* Routledge

APPENDIX A

STEM RESEARCH NOTEBOOK #12 (LESSON PLAN 2), PAGE 2

NAME_____DATE_____

The second habitat I learned about is

_____

_____

I learned . . .

_____

_____

_____

_____

_____

_____

Copyright material from Johnson, Walton & Peters-Burton (Eds.) 2024, *Habitats in the United States, Grade K,* Routledge

APPENDIX A

STEM RESEARCH NOTEBOOK #13 (LESSON PLAN 3)

NAME_____DATE_____

Habitat 1

- What is the name of the habitat?

_____

_____

- In what part of the U.S. is this habitat found? Color this area

- What is the weather like there in the winter?

_____

_____
_____

_____

Copyright material from Johnson, Walton & Peters-Burton (Eds.) 2024, *Habitats in the United States, Grade K*, Routledge

APPENDIX A

STEM RESEARCH NOTEBOOK #13, PAGE 2 (LESSON PLAN 3)

- What is the weather like there in the summer?

APPENDIX A

STEM RESEARCH NOTEBOOK #13, PAGE 3 (LESSON PLAN 3)

NAME_____DATE_____

Habitat 2

- **What is the name of the habitat?**

_____
_____

- **In what part of the U.S. is this habitat found? Color this area**

- **What is the weather like there in the winter?**

_____
_____
_____

Copyright material from Johnson, Walton & Peters-Burton (Eds.) 2024, *Habitats in the United States, Grade K,* Routledge

NATIONAL SCIENCE TEACHING ASSOCIATION

APPENDIX A

STEM RESEARCH NOTEBOOK #13, PAGE 4 (LESSON PLAN 3)

- What is the weather like there in the summer?

_____

_____

_____

_____

Copyright material from Johnson, Walton & Peters-Burton (Eds.) 2024, *Habitats in the United States, Grade K*, Routledge

APPENDIX A

STEM RESEARCH NOTEBOOK #14 (LESSON PLAN 3)

NAME_____DATE_____

My Dynamic Habitat Diorama
Diorama #1

DEFINE

Diorama must display
    Two animals that live in the habitat
    Two plants that live in the habitat

Diorama must identify
    Habitat

Write the name of the habitat here

_____

_____

LEARN

Write the names of two animals that live in the habitat

_____

_____

_____

_____

Write the names of two plants that live in the habitat

_____

_____

_____

_____

Copyright material from Johnson, Walton & Peters-Burton (Eds.) 2024, *Habitats in the United States, Grade K,* Routledge

APPENDIX A

STEM RESEARCH NOTEBOOK #14, PAGE 2 (LESSON PLAN 3)

NAME_____DATE_____

My Dynamic Habitat Diorama
Diorama #1

PLAN

Draw a picture of your habitat including the two animals and two plants

```
┌─────────────────────────────────────────────────┐
│                                                 │
│                                                 │
│                                                 │
│                                                 │
│                                                 │
│                                                 │
│                                                 │
└─────────────────────────────────────────────────┘
```

TRY: Build your diorama!

TEST/DECIDE: Does your habitat diorama include

Two animals	YES	NO
Two plants	YES	NO
The name of the habitat	YES	NO

Copyright material from Johnson, Walton & Peters-Burton (Eds.) 2024, *Habitats in the United States, Grade K*, Routledge

APPENDIX A

STEM RESEARCH NOTEBOOK #14, PAGE 3 (LESSON PLAN 3)

NAME_____DATE_____

My Dynamic Habitat Diorama
Diorama #2

DEFINE

Diorama must display
> Two animals that live in the habitat
> Two plants that live in the habitat

Diorama must identify
> Habitat

Write the name of the habitat here
_____
_____
_____

Write the names of two animals that live in the habitat
_____
_____
_____
_____
_____
_____

Write the names of two plants that live in the habitat
_____
_____
_____
_____
_____
_____

Copyright material from Johnson, Walton & Peters-Burton (Eds.) 2024, *Habitats in the United States, Grade K,* Routledge

APPENDIX A

STEM RESEARCH NOTEBOOK #14, PAGE 4 (LESSON PLAN 3)

NAME_____DATE_____

My Dynamic Habitat Diorama
Diorama #2

PLAN

Draw a picture of your habitat including the two animals and two plants

TRY: Build your diorama!

TEST/DECIDE: Does your habitat diorama include

Two animals	YES	NO
Two plants	YES	NO
The name of the habitat	YES	NO

Copyright material from Johnson, Walton & Peters-Burton (Eds.) 2024, *Habitats in the United States, Grade K*, Routledge

APPENDIX B

OBSERVATION, STEM RESEARCH NOTEBOOK, AND PARTICIPATION RUBRIC

APPENDIX B

OBSERVATION, STEM RESEARCH NOTEBOOK, AND PARTICIPATION RUBRIC

Name _____ Date _____

Categories (Components)	0 Missing or Unrelated	1 Beginning	2 Developing	3 Meets Expectations	4 Exceeds Expectation	TOTAL
Observation of listening and discussion skills	Component is missing or unrelated	Does not listen to others and shows little respect for alternative viewpoints	Occasionally listens to others but often speaks out of turn	Listens to others, only occasionally speaks out of turn, and generally accepts other points of view	Listens carefully to others, waits for turn to speak, and respects alternative viewpoints	
STEM Research Notebook	Component is missing or unrelated	Indicates little understanding of the concepts being taught	Recalls and is able to explain basic facts and concepts	Demonstrates ability to apply concepts, using information in new situations	Demonstrates a deep understanding of concepts by drawing relationships between ideas and using information to generate new ideas	
Participation	Component is missing	Does not volunteer When responding to teacher entries, comments are sometimes not relevant to the discussion	Responds to teacher entries during classroom discussions but does not volunteer	Willingly participates in classroom discussions and offers relevant comments	Contributes insightful comments and poses thoughtful questions	
TOTAL						
COMMENTS						

Copyright material from Johnson, Walton & Peters-Burton (Eds.) 2024, *Habitats in the United States, Grade K*, Routledge

APPENDIX C

CONTENT STANDARDS ADDRESSED IN THIS MODULE

NEXT GENERATION SCIENCE STANDARDS

Table C.1 (p. 145) lists the science and engineering practices, disciplinary core ideas, and crosscutting concepts this module addresses. The supported performance expectations are as follows:

K-LS1–1. Use observations to describe patterns of what plants and animals (including humans) need to survive

K-ESS3–1. Use a model to represent the relationship between the needs of different plants and animals (including humans) and the places they live

K-PS3–1. Make observations to determine the effect of sunlight on Earth's surface

APPENDIX C

Table C.1. Next Generation Science Standards (NGSS)

SCIENCE AND ENGINEERING PRACTICES
PLANNING AND CARRYING OUT INVESTIGATIONS   • Planning and carrying out investigations to answer questions or test solutions to problems in K-2 builds on prior experiences and progresses to simple investigations, based on fair tests, which provide data to support explanations or design solutions   • Plan and conduct investigations collaboratively to produce evidence to answer a question   **ANALYZING AND INTERPRETING DATA**   • Analyzing data in K-2 builds on prior experiences and progresses to collecting, recording, and sharing observations   • Use observations (firsthand or from media) to describe patterns in the natural world in order to answer scientific questions   **DEVELOPING AND USING MODELS**   • Modeling in K-2 builds on prior experiences and progresses to include using and developing models (i.e., diagram, drawing, physical replica, diorama, dramatization, storyboard) that represent concrete events or design solutions   • Use a model to represent relationships in the natural world
DISCIPLINARY CORE IDEAS
LS1.C. ORGANIZATION FOR MATTER AND ENERGY FLOW IN ORGANISMS   • All animals need food in order to live and grow. They obtain their food from plants or from other animals. Plants need water and light to live and grow   **ESS3.A. NATURAL RESOURCES**   • Living things need water, air, and resources from the land, and they live in places that have the things they need. Humans use natural resources for everything they do   **PS3.B. CONSERVATION OF ENERGY AND ENERGY TRANSFER**   • Sunlight warms Earth's surface
CROSSCUTTING CONCEPTS
PATTERNS   • Patterns in the natural world can be observed, used to describe phenomena, and used as evidence   **SYSTEMS AND SYSTEM MODELS**   • Systems in the natural and designed world have parts that work together   **CAUSE AND EFFECT**   • Events have causes that generate observable patterns

Source: NGSS Lead States. 2013. *Next Generation Science Standards: For states, by states.* Washington, DC: National Academies Press. *www.nextgenscience.org/next-generation-science-standards.*

APPENDIX C

Table C.2. Common Core Mathematics and English Language Arts (ELA) Standards

Common Core State Standards for Mathematics	Common Core State Standards for English Language Arts
MATHEMATICAL PRACTICES MP1. Make sense of problems and persevere in solving them MP2. Reason abstractly and quantitatively MP3. Construct viable arguments and critique the reasoning of others MP4. Model with mathematics MP5. Use appropriate tools strategically MP6. Attend to precision MP7. Look for and make use of structure MP8. Look for and express regularity in repeated reasoning **MATHEMATICAL CONTENT** K.CC.B.4. Understand the relationship between numbers and quantities; connect counting to cardinality K.CC.B.4a. When counting objects, say the number names in the standard order, pairing each object with one and only one number name and each number name with one and only one object K.CC.B.4b. Understand that the last number name said tells the number of objects counted. The number of objects is the same regardless of their arrangement or the order in which they were counted K.CC.B.4c. Understand that each successive number name refers to a quantity that is one larger K.CC.C.6. Identify whether the number of objects in one group is greater than, less than, or equal to the number of objects in another group, for example, by using matching and counting strategies K.CC.C.7. Compare two numbers between 1 and 10 presented as written numerals K.MD.A.1. Describe measurable attributes of objects, such as length or weight. Describe several measurable attributes of a single object K.MD.A.2. Directly compare two objects with a measurable attribute in common, to see which object has "more of"/"less of" the attribute, and describe the difference. For example, directly compare the heights of two children and describe one child as taller/shorter	**READING STANDARDS** RI.K.1. With prompting and support, ask and answer questions about key details in a text RI.K.3. With prompting and support, describe the connection between two individuals, events, ideas, or pieces of information in a text **WRITING STANDARDS** W.K.2. Use a combination of drawing, dictating, and writing to compose informative/explanatory texts in which they name what they are writing about and supply some information about the topic W.K.5. With guidance and support from adults, respond to questions and suggestions from peers and add details to strengthen writing as needed W.K.7. Participate in shared research and writing projects (for example, explore a number of books by a favorite author and express opinions about them) **SPEAKING AND LISTENING STANDARDS** SL.K.1. Participate in collaborative conversations with diverse partners about *kindergarten topics and texts* with peers and adults in small and larger groups SL.K.3. Ask and answer questions in order to seek help, get information, or clarify something that is not understood SL.K.5. Add drawings or other visual displays to descriptions as desired to provide additional detail

Continued

APPENDIX C

Table C.2. (continued)

Common Core State Standards for Mathematics	Common Core State Standards for English Language Arts
K.MD.B.3. Classify objects into given categories; count the numbers of objects in each category and sort the categories by count K.CC.A.1. Count to 100 by ones and by tens K.CC.A.2. Count forward beginning from a given number within the known sequence (instead of having to begin at 1) K.CC.A.3. Write numbers from 0 to 20. Represent a number of objects with a written numeral 0–20 (with 0 representing a count of no objects) K.CC.B.5. Count to answer "how many?" questions about as many as 20 things arranged in a line, a rectangular array, or a circle, or as many as 10 things in a scattered configuration; given a number from 1–20, count out that many objects	

Source: National Governors Association Center for Best Practices and Council of Chief State School Officers (NGAC and CCSSO). 2010. *Common core state standards.* Washington, DC: NGAC and CCSSO.

Table C.3. National Association for the Education of Young Children (NAEYC) Standards

NAEYC Curriculum Content Area for Cognitive Development: Science and Technology
2.G.02. Children are provided with varied opportunities and materials to learn key content and principles of science
2.G.03. Children are provided with varied opportunities and materials that encourage them to use the five senses to observe, explore, and experiment with scientific phenomena
2.G.04. Children are provided with varied opportunities to use simple tools to observe objects and scientific phenomena
2.G.05. Children are provided with varied opportunities and materials to collect data and to represent and document their findings (for example, through drawing or graphing)
2.G.06. Children are provided with varied opportunities and materials that encourage them to think, questions, and reason about observed and inferred phenomena
2.G.07. Children are provided with varied opportunities and materials that encourage them to discuss scientific concepts in everyday conversation
2.G.08. Children are provided with varied opportunities and materials that help them learn and use scientific terminology and vocabulary associated with the content areas
2.H.02. All children have opportunities to access technology that they can use
2.H.03. Technology is used to extend learning within the classroom and integrate and enrich the curriculum

Source: National Association for the Education of Young Children (NAEYC). 2005. *NAEYC early childhood program standards and accreditation criteria: The mark of quality in early childhood education.* Washington, DC: NAEYC.

APPENDIX C

Table C.4. 21st Century Skills From the Framework for 21st Century Learning

21st Century Skills	Learning Skills and Technology Tools	Teaching Strategies	Evidence of Success
Interdisciplinary Themes	Economic, business, and entrepreneurial literacy Health literacy Environmental literacy	• Provide students with the opportunity to investigate sustainable systems by exploring various habitats in the context of the economics of everyday life and the business industry (for example, housing, communities, how human needs are met in society)	• Students will compare and contrast their prior and current experiences with various habitats in relation to climate and the animals, plants, and people that live in those habitats in the context of everyday life
Learning and innovation skills	Creativity and Innovation Critical thinking and problem solving Communication and collaboration	• Facilitate creativity and innovation through the creation of dioramas and a reference guide that describes various habitats and their similarities and differences • Facilitate critical thinking and problem solving through use of the EDP and having students make observations about their surroundings • Support students in communication skills both within groups and in making presentations	• Students acquire and use deeper content knowledge as they work to complete their dioramas and their reference guides • Students work collaboratively and communicate effectively in teams to complete and present a group project
Information, media and technology skills	Information literacy Media literacy Information communication and technology literacy	• Engage students in guided practice and scaffolding strategies through the use of developmentally appropriate books, videos, and websites to advance their knowledge	• Students acquire and use deeper content knowledge as they work to complete the reference guides
Life and career skills	Flexibility and adaptability Initiative and self-direction Social and cross-cultural skills Productivity and accountability Leadership and responsibility	• Facilitate student collaborative teamwork to foster life and career skills	• Throughout this module, students collaborate to conduct research and work on their group project

Source: Partnership for 21st Century Learning. 2015. Framework for 21st Century Learning. www.p21.org/our-work/p21-framework.

APPENDIX C

Table C.5. English Language Development Standards

English Language Development Standards: Grades K (WIDA, 2020)
ELD Standard 1: Social and Instructional Language
Multilingual learners narrate, inform, explain, and argue.
ELD Standard 2: Language for Language Arts
Multilingual learners will interpret and construct informational texts in language arts with prompting and support
ELD Standard 3: The Language of Mathematics
Multilingual learners will interpret and construct mathematical informational texts with prompting and support
ELD Standard 4: The Language of Science
Multilingual learners will interpret and construct scientific informational texts and explanations
ELD Standard 5: The Language of Social Studies
Multilingual learners will interpret and construct informational texts in social studies

Source: WIDA. (2020). *WIDA English language development standards framework, 2020 edition: Kindergarten–grade 12.* Board of Regents of the University of Wisconsin System. *https://wida.wisc.edu/sites/default/files/resource/WIDA-ELD-Standards-Framework-2020.pdf*

INDEX

Page numbers in **bold** refer to tables; page numbers in *italics* refer to figures.

5E model 12

A

accountability 5, **149**
activities 10–14, 16, 17, **28,** 50–5, 71–5, 86–9, 96–7; and assessment 14, 113; and differentiated instruction 29; and notebooks 18; safety considerations 19, 31, 41, 63; and standards 2; STEM focused 6; and team work 9
Amazing Habitats! **34, 35,** 39–60
Animals at Home 34, 40
argument 15, **42, 64, 83, 93,** 147
assessment 1, 12–16, 18, **28,** 29, 31–4, 57, 77, 90, 99; comprehensive 14; formative 14–16, 27, **32–3,** 113; role in *STEM Road Map Curriculum Series* 13–16; strategies 9; summative 14–16, **32–3;** *see also* evaluation
assignments 29

B

background information 45–8, 67, 70, 85, 95
best practice pedagogy 9
blueprints 11, 15
brainstorming **28,** 67, 96, 98

C

careers 31, 46–7, 77
causality *see* cause and effect
cause and effect 2, 3, **25, 42, 64, 82, 93,** 120, **146**
CCSS ELA see Common Core Standards for English Language Arts
CCSS see Common Core Standards for Mathematics
challenges 1–2, 6, 12, 24, **36,** 46, 96; *see also* zoo habitat challenge
clarification 17, **44, 65,** 84
climate 3, 24, **25, 33, 44,** 46, 51, 52, 61, 73, 80, **85,** 87–8, 91, 97, 99, **149;** *see also* weather

Common Core Standards for English Language Arts (CCSS ELA) 2, **43–4, 65, 83–4, 94–5, 147**
Common Core Standards for Mathematics (CCSS) 2, 18, 41, **42–3, 64–5, 83, 93–4, 147, 148**
communication 5, 6, 10, 11, 45, **149**
community members 3
compacting 29
concepts 1–4, 6, 10, 12, 15, 18, 24, 27, 29, **44,** 47, 48, 84–6, **95, 144,** 145, 148; crosscutting **42, 64, 66, 69, 82, 93, 146**
conceptual knowledge 6
conceptual misunderstandings 27; *see also* misconceptions
constructivism 16
consumers 3
content standards 24, 41–4, 63–6, 72, 82–5, 92–5, 145–150
context 5–6, 9–10, 12, 29, **149**
core ideas 3, 15, **42, 63, 82, 92, 146**
Council of State Science Supervisors (CSSS) 19
CSSS *see* Council of State Science Supervisors
cyclical learning processes 16

D

data 11, 13, 15, 17, 30, **32, 42, 44,** 61, **64, 66, 82, 84, 89,** 93, **95, 146**
definition **44, 45,** 50, **66,** 67, 68, **85,** 95
deliverables 31, **32**
design 4–7, 9–13, 17, 24, **28,** 29–30, **33, 42,** 61, **64, 66,** 67–71, 73–77, 79, 80, **82–3, 93, 146;** collaborative 29
designers 10–11
diagrams 4, 11, **42, 64, 83, 93, 146**
differentiation 1, **25–6,** 29–30, 113
dioramas **31–3, 36,** 80–6, 88–90, 92, 96, 99, **149**
discussion 7, 13, 17, 24, 25, **26, 34, 36,** 50–2, 71, 74, 87, 96–9, **144**

Habitats in the United States, Grade K

INDEX

E
Earth processes 4
Earth-Sun-Moon cycles 4
ecosystems 4
EDP *see* engineering design process
educational reform 5
elaboration 12, 16, 18, 56–7, 76–7, 89–90, 99
electronic notebooks 13
engagement 12, 16, 17, **28,** 50, 55, 71–3, 86–8, 96–7
engineering 2, 9–10, 67–9, **82–3, 93;** practices **64;** *see also* engineering design process
engineering design process (EDP) 6, 9–10, **35,** 46, 61, 67–9, 74–5, 79, 113; *see also* engineering
English language arts (ELA) 2, **43–4,** 52, 72–3, 75, 88, 97–9
English Language Development Standards **150**
English language learners 30–31
environment 3–5, 15–16, 29–30, **36, 48,** 50, 52, 54, **70,** 98–9, **149**
environmental learning contexts 29
evaluation 12, 18, **28,** 57, 77, 90, 99; *see also* assessment
expectations 2, 5, 11, 12, **144,** 145
experimenting 10
explanation 12, 14, 16, 18, **42, 48,** 56, **64, 69–70,** 76, **85,** 89, 98–99, **146, 150**
exploration 2, 12, 14, 16, 18, 71, 113
expression 5

F
feedback 4, 12, 14, **28,** 68
flowcharts 11
Framework for 21st Century Learning 1, 2, **44, 66, 84, 95, 149**
Framework for STEM Integration in the Classroom 6

G
global citizens 3
goals 14, 23–4, 31, 39, 61, 80, 91
grades 12, 13, **150**
graphic organizers 13
graphic representations 30, 67
graphs 4, 89
grouping 21, 29, 99
group tasks **26**

H
heat transfer 4

I
images 30, 96
innovation 2, 3, **95, 149**
integrated approach 5–6
interdisciplinary themes **44, 66, 64, 95, 149**
investigation **28,** 29, 53, 73–5, 88, 97, **146**

J
journaling 13, 17, 29

K
kindergarteners 45
knowledge 10, 17, 99; application 12, 16, 18, **25–6,** 56–7, 76–7, 89; conceptual 6; of core ideas 15; demonstration of 12, **31;** foundational 27; imprecise 27; prerequisite **25–6,** 29; reconstruction 27
Know, Want to Know, Learned (KWL) 27, 47, 48, 50, 51, 53, 71–3, 87–8, 96–7
KWL *see* Know, Want to Know, Learned

L
laboratory practicals 15
language 30–1, 45
learning 14, 16–18, 68; and assessment 14; cycle 9, 16; from experience 10; from failure 6; and innovation **95, 149;** and inquiry 17; prior **28;** problem based 1, 6, 9, 29; project based 1, 9, 29; reflection on 18; self-regulated 16–18, 27–8; skills 15, **149;** and the *STEM Road Map Curriculum Series* 5, 113–14; theories 16; transformation 113–14
lesson plans: Lesson Plan 1 39–60; Lesson Plan 2 61–79; Lesson Plan 3 80–90; Lesson Plan 4 91–112
Let's Explore Habitats throughout the United States **35, 36,** 80–90
Let's Explore Our Local Habitat! **35,** 61–79
listening **94, 147**
literature 29

M
maps 72; assessment 15–16
matching tests 14
materials 11, 40–1, 61–3, 80–1, 91–2
mathematics 2, 4–5, 51–2, 57, 63–5, 72–3, 75–7, **83,** 87–9, **93–4,** 113, **147–8**

INDEX

meaningful learning 16
measurement 11, **26**
memoranda 11
mentoring 30
mentors 17
misconceptions 13, 14, 16, 27, 45, 48, 69–70, 85–6, 95, 113; vernacular 27
modeling **26,** 30
models **146**
module, timeline **34–6**
monitoring 17, **28,** 31
motivation 16, **28,** 45
multiple choice tests 14
My Dynamic Habitat Diorama **32, 33, 36,** 81, 85, 88
My Habitat Reference Manual **32**

N

National Academy of Engineering 2
National Association for the Education of Young Children **44, 66, 84, 94, 148**
National Science Teachers Association (NSTA) 19
Next Generation Science Standards (NGSS) 2, 18, 41, **63–4, 82–3, 92–3,** 145, **146**
NGSS *see Next Generation Science Standards*
nonscientific beliefs 27
notebooks 11, **26**; electronic 13; research 12–13, 17, 18, 24, **31, 32,** 48, 50–2, 54–6, 61, 73–6, 88–9, 115–41, **144**
NSTA *see* National Science Teachers Association
numeracy **26**

O

objectives 6, 23–4, 39, **41,** 61, 63, 80, **82,** 91, **92**
observation 17, 99, 120, **144**
Our First Talk About Our Impact on the Environment **36**
Our Habitat Reference Guides **36**
Our Nature Walk **36**
Our Neighborhood Habitats **32,** 73–4
Our Neighborhood Walking Tour 62
outcomes 31

P

participation 49, 57, 77, 90, 99, **144**
pedagogy 1, 7, 9; problem based 6
planning 11, 67, 68, 71–3, 86–90, 96–7, **146**
policies 19, 49, 71

preconceived notions 27
predictions 17, **26,** 47–8, 52, 54, 56, 120
preparation 40, 48, 52, 70–2, 86–7, 89, 96
presentations 4, 11, 13, 29–33, 89–90, 96
previewing 17, 48, 86
probes 27
problem-based learning 1, 6, 9, 29
problem-based pedagogy 6
problem scoping 9, 10
process skills 15
professional development 114
project-based learning 1, 6, 9, 29
projects 6, **43, 65, 84, 94, 147**
prompts 13
prototypes 11, 113

Q

questions 5, 12, 13, 15, 17, 25, **26, 28,** 39, **42–4,** 45, 61, 64–6, 73–4, 80, **82–4,** 91, **93–5,** 97, 99, **120, 144, 146–8**
quizzes 14, 15

R

reading 10, **26,** 29–30, 37, **43,** 47–8, 52, **65,** 76, **83, 94, 147**; aloud **26,** 47–8
Reference Guide for Habitats 33
regions 68–9
representations 4, 11, 30–1
represented world, the 2, 3–4
research notebook 12–13, 17, 18, 24, **31, 32,** 48, 50, 51, 52, 54–6, 61, 73–6, 88–9, 115–41, **144**
resources 37; Internet 57–8, 77–8, 90, 100
rock cycle 4
rules 19, 25, 45, 50, 87

S

safety 18–19, 31, 41, 63, 81
scaffolding 1, 2, 9, 13, 29, **149**
schematics 11
schools 1, 6, 7, 114
science 2, 5, 72–3, 76, **82–3,** 87–9, **93,** 96–9; classes 50, 56; practices 15, **42, 64, 82–3,** 145, **146;** teaching 5
science, technology, engineering, and mathematics *see* STEM
self-reflection 18
self-regulated learning (SRL) 16–18, 27–8
sensory support 30
Shelter Me activity **28, 32, 33, 35,** 62–3, 67, 71, 73–5, 130
situated cognition 16

INDEX

skills 1, 10, 17; carer 149; communication 45; demonstration of 12; development 12; higher level thinking 14; information, media and technology 149; language 45; learning 15, 149; life **149**; listening **26**; mastery 29; process 15; required 25; speaking **26**; SRL 18; 21st century 6, **149**
social studies 1, 2, 5, 6, 23, 29, 50–6, 72–3, 76, 87–9, 96–9, 113, 150
solutions 5, 9, 10, 11, 17, **42**, **64**, 67–8, 83, **93**, **146**
speaking **94**, **147**
SRL *see* self-regulated learning
standards 2, 4, 6, 24, 41–4, 63–6, 72, 82–5, 92–5, 145–50
STEM (science, technology, engineering, and mathematics): framework for classroom integration 6; meaning 5; need for integrated approach 5–6; potential misconceptions 27; research notebook 12–13, 17, 18, 24, **31**, **32**, 48, 50, 51, 52, 54–6, 61, 73–6, 88–9, 115–41, **144**; safety in 18–19; *see also STEM Road Map Curriculum* Series
STEM Road Map Curriculum Series: and Framework for STEM Integration in the Classroom 6; and learning 113–14; need for 7; overview 1; role of assessment in 13–16; strategies used in 9–19
storyboards 11
STEM Road Map: overview 1–7; self-regulated learning theory in 16–18, 27–8; strategies used in 9–19, 29–31
STEM Road Map 9–19strategies 9–19, 113; for differentiating instruction 29–30; for English Language Learners 30–1; in the student-centered pedagogy 6
sustainability 4
systems 2, 4–5, **42**, 46, 64, 67, **82**, **93**, 113; sustainable 23, **146, 149**

T

tasks 15, **26, 31, 57,** 67, 77, 90, 99
T-chart **25**
teachers 5, 12–19, 30, 49, 77, 86, 88, 90, 99, 113, **144**; background information 45–8, 67–9; and the curriculum 1; dealing with misconceptions 27; and ELLs 30; and mentoring 30; resources for 7, 37; safety responsibilities 18–19; and SRL learning components **28**; and vocabulary 41, 63, 82, 92, 95
teaching: and accountability 5; strategies **149**; time for 5
teamwork 6, 10, 11, **26,** 30, 46, **149**
technical briefs 11
temperatures **26, 45,** 49, 52, 89
templates 24, **32–3,** 50, 92, 96–7, 115–42
testing 5, 10, 11, 67, **70;** *see also* tests
tests 11, 14, **42, 64, 146;** *see also* testing
themes 1–5, **44, 66, 84, 95, 149**
thinking 3–5, 12, 14, 16, 45, 70; critical **149**
thought processes **26**
timeline **34–6**

U

understanding 3–5, 17, **25, 26, 27, 28,** 29–30, **33,** 45, 48, 51, 67, 69, 80, 86, **114**

V

vernacular misconceptions 27
videos 25, **34, 35,** 48, 72, 98
vocabulary 30, **34,** 41, **44–5,** 47–8, 50, 52, 63, **66,** 82, 84, **85,** 92, **95, 118,** 148

W

weather 4, 24, 37, 39, **44–5,** 52, **66,** 74–5, **85,** 87, 91, 96–8, 124, 129, 130, 134–7; chart **34,** 40, 49, 51, **59,** 89
Wonder Worms habitats **32, 34,** 40, 53–4, 56, 120
worksheets 14
worms **32, 34–5,** 40, 41, 46, 49, 53–7, 120
writing **26,** 37, **43, 52,** 65, 77, **84, 94, 147**

Z

zoo displays 24, 50, 91, 92
Zoo Habitat Challenge 24, **36,** 46, 50, 71, 86, 91–112

For Product Safety Concerns and Information please contact our EU representative GPSR@taylorandfrancis.com
Taylor & Francis Verlag GmbH, Kaufingerstraße 24, 80331 München, Germany

www.ingramcontent.com/pod-product-compliance
Lightning Source LLC
Chambersburg PA
CBHW060301240426

43661CB00060B/2856